How to apply innovation to your activities through green business

In this book I want to talk to you about various themes, only apparently divergent from each other.

I will also tell you about some windows that are opening in the market (you will find a hint to the theme of books concerning specific product categories for example), I will also talk to you about "work from home" and how to build a profitable job having your place of work in the place where you live, it is not simply a matter of smart working, a definition that has been gaining ground in our vocabulary for some time and recently taken up by politics due to the pandemic that hit the world, that of covid-19.

You will also find the environmental problem among the pages and scrolling through the book, a theme that gives the title to this ebook, and I chose it because it is a central theme today, it has always been, but currently it is becoming more and more.

This theme will lead you to what is happening in entire areas of the world by observing how policies are focusing on this issue which today appears more than ever decisive and should be addressed without too many turns of words and in a perspective of change, including economic change that reconverting the model that has so far been implemented and based mainly on poorly distributed wealth and an environment treated as "ara" to be exploited without thinking about the consequences of this abuse.

Finally in the last part of the book I will deal with the theme of your own economic development, there are many success stories that have been able to combine an innovative approach to the need to make yourself known. Have you ever heard of Homeless to billionaire and Stressless success?

But I don't want to limit myself to bringing the stories to your knowledge, however important it is to understand how each person involved started from themselves to often create real empires, I will analyze the methods and resources that have allowed these people to become millionaires and I will quote a woman who has created a truly inspirational book, Stress Less Success.

Topic index

The non-fiction market: possibilities and resources

Forget the books that deal with the theme of work, today the market is asking for non-fiction, a definition that can leave the most perplexed, since potentially everything could fall into this category.

Below we will see together what is the definition of non-fiction in national and international publishing.

Entrepreneurs are inundated with books that deal (mainly but not only) with the theme of business consultancy, but in the job it is important to be informed as it is to have a balance between abstraction and inspiration, and to inspire non-fiction they are ideal readings that stimulate ideas creative.

Reading done for personal pleasure therefore stimulates creativity but also practical action which is closely linked to a creative approach.

The truth is, reading non-fiction can be as fruitful for your business as reading a business book.

Do not you believe it?

We will soon prove to you the truthfulness of this statement.

For busy entrepreneurs, taking the time to sit down to read a book of several pages may seem like an unwarranted indulgence, how many times do you think books are to be relegated to something that goes beyond the work performance of individuals? Unfortunately, there are preconceptions about this aspect that are difficult to eradicate.

Yet there are some very good reasons to read for work too, which could be useful for your business. Here is a list of the reasons why reading and business should go together:

1. Reading can inspire more creative thinking.

There is nothing like intellectual digression (which allows you more effective attention later) to help come up with new ideas.

If you go to observe all the holistic advice provided to optimize the times and ways of working in the company, certainly one of the ones you will find most frequently is to think more creatively taking time for yourself and moving away from the great challenges to elaborate them to the best. Distance inspires innovation.

2. Look from another perspective and then see what you don't know yet.

Curiosity is a potential engine for inspiration, having an open mind allows you to stimulate new perspectives, evolved points of view and to do this, a book or a series of books not purely focused on business strategies but on other themes broaden the perspectives stimulating curiosity that triggers potential ideas.

The sign of intelligence is curiosity, and there is no better way to inspire you than to learn to read stories about things you have little knowledge of.

Learning is the embrace of the unknown.

3. Return to the priorities.

Reading and immersing yourself in a great story can help you disconnect from everyday stress and from all those tests of daily life that you constantly face.

Regarding your business or not, reading offers you a necessary and therefore important perspective on what is truly relevant by helping you concentrate your strategy, and promoting optimal planning.

However, keep in mind that not all non-fiction is created equal.

Publishing in Italy moves constantly but it is not an economic area of such great interest, unfortunately.

Instead, the steps that this publishing is doing abroad are interesting.

Italy today (or rather the publishing market sector in Italy) is followed and visited by international publishers such as HarperCollins, which has an important role on the international chessboard, or medium-small ones such as the newly formed Blackie editions.

This market is interested in exploring the foreign publishing sectors (including Italy) by moving personally and broadening its horizons.

But which are the Italian publishing groups that are getting more acquisitions?

Two above all:

> *Bompiani*

> *Giunti*

In recent years Giunti has certainly been one of the publishing groups that has made its mark most notably in the field of acquisitions together with Bompiani, and therefore it is not surprising that they have also moved internationally.

Very recently the news emerged that Giunti acquired 20% of Quarto group, an English publishing group which in turn had and continues to move internationally, and which has offices in the United States, Australia and Hong Kong.

This 20% therefore has a considerable weight given that Quarto group is particularly active in the sector of illustrated books intended for the adult public with an important area dedicated to the children's sector.

This acquisition is part of the history of the Italian publisher and at the same time with an eye to the future and to new markets that are establishing themselves by demonstrating how reading and the use of certain themes have changed, taking into account that through this move Giunti enters thanks to a considerable investment in the English-speaking market and in others.

In fact, it should be remembered that Quarto has a market in more than 50 countries, translating its texts into more than 40 languages.

The chairman of the Sergio Giunti group claims that:

«We are aware of the evolutions that new technologies impose on the book market and we are working on the publishing house of tomorrow which will necessarily have an international horizon.

We pay great attention to the possibilities offered by Quarto's global distribution, to the development of new markets also but not only in the Anglo-Saxon context.

We look with great curiosity to China, India, Southeast Asia. For publishing there are still endless opportunities. "

Given this brief (yet intense) overview of Italian publishing that has moved with Giunti towards a specific address by expanding its reference market and with attention to the requests of the public (given the issues, you understand what the public is choosing by addressing publishing).

We also understand the desire to start taking a few more steps outside the borders of the Italian state; on the English side, there was certainly a strong interest in the great experience that a group like Giunti brings to the table.

Quarto's CEO and majority shareholder, Chuk Kin Lau confirms:

"Giunti's experience in creating content, selling and distributing non-fiction books, both wholesale and retail, is remarkable.

Quarto is looking forward to collaborating with Giunti in the joint development of non-fiction books in English, for sale in the traditional and emerging markets of the world ».

To reinforce this new relationship, Andrea Giunti was given a permanent place on the board of the Quarto Group.

Now we have to wait for the next few months in which we will begin to see the practical effects of this new international publishing agreement.

Particularly interesting will be the books that will be born from the joint development mentioned by Chuk Kin Lau, and in general the coeditions, given that the latter turns out to be a widely used tool precisely in the context of children's books, in particular in those illustrated, and in books that have a high iconographic content, as can be some types of manuals - and translations.

It is easy to understand how extremely interesting new potential markets are being defined.

Among the themes that stood out in the sale of books internationally, certainly that of the struggle for the emancipation of women and against gender violence was a very significant and important theme of 2019 both in novels and essays.

Also in this case, I would like to point out some that are also available to users on the Italian market:

> *Sorcières: the puissance invaincue des femmes by Mona Chollet.*

Very important text that traces in the Malleus Maleficarum and in the accusation of witchcraft the origin of the folding of women into a narrow (stereotyped and conveyed at the mainstream) home space, with the consequent renunciation of their ambitions and desires.

> *Klubben by Matilda Gustavsson.*

Very important text that traces in the Malleus Maleficarum and in the accusation of witchcraft the origin of the folding of women into a narrow (stereotyped and conveyed at the mainstream) home space, with the consequent renunciation of their ambitions and desires.

> *Het ultieme mannenkookboek.*

A fun recipe book aimed at men of all kinds. This is to be considered as a real manual that provides the basic knowledge useful for preparing various types of dishes with various tips and suggestions for cooking and eating with pleasure.

Javier Castillo ranks at the top of the Spanish rankings for 2020 and has achieved this position for two consecutive months.

While there are eight titles in the top 10 of the Netherlands and which come from the United Kingdom as texts.

Italy instead rediscovers the Harry Potter saga.

Instead in China in the ranking of this country, there is a Japanese author with his three novels.

Entering the merits of this ranking let's see the and the protagonists, of some we already know something, but of the others much less.

For example, many and many do not know that the career of the Spanish author Javier Castillo began in 2014 in the immense group of self-published authors on Amazon.

And it was on Amazon that he sold his debut novel El día que se loi cordura today translated and adapted by HarperCollins Italia, his first work sold 45,000 copies.

After an offer from the Penguin Random House, his work was published not only in his home country, but also in Italy and Turkey.

Currently this author has sold a total of 650,000 copies.

The fourth novel he published, entitled: La chica de nieve (1st in Spain for the second month in a row) was published in March by Suma de Letras (Penguin Random House).

The story starts in 1998 in a terrible scenario feared by all parents. Kiera Templeton, 3, disappears into the crowd during the Thanksgiving Day parade in New York, and despite prompt and detailed research she is not found.

In 2003, on the day of Kiera's eighth birthday, her parents received a package containing a videotape with a one-minute recording where Kiera's voice is heard.

The new evidence leads journalism student Miren Triggs to become passionate about the case and start a parallel investigation.

Like many others who operate and offer their creativity in the cultural sector, Javier Castillo was forced to stop his promotional tour due to the covid-19, but has recently managed to inspire 60,000 fans in Europe, the United States and South America by creating a live reading session on his Instagram profile.

Moving on to another important signature it must be said that the general classification in the Netherlands in April 2020 saw 8 titles in the top 10 originating in the United Kingdom, and all with a female target.

Six of these texts are by Lucinda Riley, 5 texts fall into the saga Le sette sorelle and De vlinderkamer (in Italian La stanza delle farfalle, for Giunti Editore), with whom she secures the first place.

One title each has been published by the author duo Nicci French (4th place) and Jill Mansell (5th place). These are two Dutch titles in the top ten positions: an essay by the famous cabaret artist Paulien Cornelisse and a crime novel by Suzanne Vermeer, pseudonym behind which hides an author who is still unknown, and who does not even know the publisher AW Bruna.

This mix is the reflection of very profound changes in the bestselling segment: the traditional careers of authors with a personal profile that tends to stand out and an ever growing recognition between the public and the media are becoming less and less widespread.

They are replaced with "brands" of the authors who develop more marketable series around a figure or as a whole.

Xander Uitgevers, the Dutch publisher of Riley, founded the house in 2012 to cover this area. Free from "traditional gender boundaries", Xander's offering tends to appeal to "eclectic readers of the 21st century".

For 2020, a collapse of the book market is expected (and is already taking place unfortunately), with losses of up to 900 million (in Italy).

The Italian Publishers' Association recently presented sales figures, and here is what emerged:

> *January-April 2020: minus 134 million euros.*

Data relating to the blocking of new securities issued is also estimated:

> *January-April: minus 91.1% of new titles coming out*

According to many, it is moving from a health emergency to a cultural emergency.

The publishing industry is undergoing an extremely heavy economic collapse in Italy, and many in the post lockdown are asking for targeted interventions before it is too late.

Ricardo Franco Levi, president of the Italian Publishers Association (IEA), during the presentation of the sales data of the first four months of 2020 that shocked the publishing world with various closures that occurred both during the forced restrictions and at Following phase 2 envisaged by the government, it estimated an overall loss for the end of 2020 of between 650 and 900 million euros out of a total turnover of 3.2 billion euros.

If we rely on Nielsen estimates, the publishing market varies, that is to say, of fiction and non-fiction in bookstores, online stores and large-scale distribution organized from January 1st until May 3rd of this year, it has collected a net loss of 90.3 million of Euro.

If the data relating to sales made outside the channels detected by the research institutes are also added, such as:

➤ *stationery stores,*

➤ *direct sales,*

➤ *exhibitions,*

➤ *specialist bookstores,*

➤ *university libraries.*

The economic loss increases to around 134 million euros.

To this must be added the block of changes as previously noted.

In the period from March 16 to May 3, the publishers distributed by the major national groups blocked 91.1 percent of the outputs, while the production of ebooks increased by 28.6%.

In this period of time the buying habits have also changed, obviously people have gone towards a greater purchase on the web.

There is this analysis provided by the IEA, the same that says how the bookstores that have decided to limit a drop in revenues which in some cases has reached 90% of the turnover compared to 2019 are the ones that have developed new ideas and strategies on the net and on the territory, some examples in this sense were:

➤ *Incentive and / or opening of sites to continue selling,*

➤ *a home delivery sometimes made, even by bicycle, by the booksellers themselves,*

➤ *comparison and dialogue with readers on social networks,*

> ➤ *platforms like Facebook updated more than usual,*

> ➤ *direct Instagram to replace them with presentations that could no longer be done.*

If something good has emerged from this virus it is that we will no longer hear about paper versus digital and independent booksellers compared to those that are not.

Even if the problems persist and have worsened due to the pandemic.

In a scenario of this kind, it is essential, as Levi also argues, to remain united, going to avoid losing publishing houses, bookstores, authors, translators, distributors or other protagonists of the editorial chain, going back to the simplest gesture there is: l purchase of a text.

Here are Levi's words on this stage:

"In agreement with the requests that other European publishers and other booksellers will also make to their ministers of culture, we ask the Italian government for a million one-hundred euro purchase vouchers to distribute to families with children of five or six years of age, to spend in physical bookstores. "

The requests are on the plate, and the Italian publishing, being part of an international publishing (read globalization of the markets to understand the meaning of this association), needing to start again makes its requests and plans its initiatives for the immediate future.

What is non-fiction?

Non-fiction is a literary category that is not always understood in its meaning.

Non-fiction has been a buzzword since 2014.

The distances between the styles must however take into account the fact that in Italy (and beyond) there is a long tradition of works that could, rightly, enter the genre, despite this country there has never been a specific mention of non-fiction, starting from Primo Levi, passing through Arbasino and Oriana Fallaci, going as far as the previously mentioned Saviano.

So what is this non-fiction?

Someone wonders (and is a legitimate question) if it is all that cannot be called a novel?

In order not to be defined as a novel, it is enough that a work does not have a plot, but attention is paid to the absence of a plot in the classic sense?

These are perhaps some of the questions from which David Shields' Hunger for Reality was born, a text now dated 10 years and released in Italy by Fazi, who has become one of the cornerstones on which to base the non-fiction of recent years, and going to arouse an animated discussion within the American (and international) literary landscape.

In this book Shields (also the author of the excellent biography of JD Salinger published by ISBN Edizioni) makes a real collection of more than six hundred reflections and aphorisms that aim to underline and support an extreme need of contemporary literature to bear witness, revealing reality and authenticity, which can be expressed without restrictions of form and content.

In Italy talking about non-fiction today still has notes of novelty, avant-garde, the readers of John D'Agata and Emmanuel Carrère are led to be pleased with themselves in leafing through the books of authors of the genre feeling part of a not-well-defined elite of readers of the well known and attractive "niche".

But at the same time from other parts of the world such as in the United States there is a strong tradition of the genre properly defined as non-fiction: from the classic Death in the afternoon by Hemingway to the non-fiction works of David Foster Wallace, a true innovator of the genre with books like A funny thing that I will never do again (minimum fax), Consider lobster, Short interviews with lousy men and Of meat and nothing (all Einaudi Stile Libero).

Non-fiction wants to reveal the mainstream, and often succeeds in bringing to the reader and reader a different, if not completely opposed to that mainstream, testimonies, tests, analysis scenarios.

In this sense, it is an avant-garde that gradually over time has become established precisely for its antithetical character to a specific way of narrating social and cultural events.

Organized home office: swing trade

Among the sectors to be kept under observation as they are becoming increasingly popular, there is also that of domestic trading that generates workstations all over the world.

If you are a trader, you know how important it is to practice this profession of trader from home when it comes to focusing and producing on the overall and general level.

Have you ever wondered how others organize their businesses?

I asked him and in addition to studying and updating myself on the subject, I asked (the best source for learning techniques and secrets) to the operators to share their work experiences from home.

Meanwhile, the image!

Well, organizing work from home especially if we talk about organized home swing trade requires a series of precautions, the work environment is precisely organized.

> ➢ *Multiple monitors*

> ➢ *Creative PC furniture for trading from home*

It is understood that a comfortable environment allows for a more serene job, so concentrating on the image in this case becomes more than useful.

Do you want some advice to improve the work experience and the organization of the work space at home?

So I want to give you some tips to optimize your home environment and to carry out home trading, whether you are a day trader, a swing trader or an active self-employed investor, these tips apply to all of you.

N ° 1: Try to match the configuration of your monitor to your trading style

For many and many traders it is important to be able to interface with multiple monitors, but these must not be too many, balance is also necessary according to those who have experienced this modus operandi.

This approach allows you to track multiple tickers and compare related and unrelated information such as the performance of the same security over different time periods.

Personally, I was struck by the fact that many people who work with a single screen or a laptop did it on the basis of simplicity and portability ', so in this case you have to take into account how you are and what you can actually follow on one or multiple screens.

Many screens can actually distract and make you lose concentration, you have to take this into account if you think it could compromise your work.

N ° 2: Make sure you have a fast and stable Internet connection at your disposal

To work from home (with whatever job you have to do but especially if you operate on the financial markets for which constant monitoring must be a practice) a stable connection is very important.

Nobody wants to lose a trade because of data that takes too long to load or because of a connection that goes dark at the worst possible time.

Until recently we tended to recommend a wired Ethernet connection, but the reliability of wireless has improved significantly in the meantime, which is why if it is available, you should pay extra for a higher speed that will be guaranteed by the your supplier.

N ° 3: Practice on yourself going to minimize distractions

If you work from an office or home, however, you are in a separate room that (should) be isolated from the daily activities of other family members.

Set up a schedule for yourself for your trading job, a schedule that will be valid for each day, week or month and let others know that you won't be available during that period.

When the time comes for your trading operations, turn off your cell phone and close the door so you can concentrate on finding low risk and high potential opportunities using the trading strategy you have adopted.

No. 4: You must be comfortable or comfortable

Choosing furnishing accessories to stay in the best possible position falls on your health but also on how you manage work from home by doing your best you will achieve your goals in the best way.

You can choose for example an avant-garde ergonomic chair or a classic office chair that allows you to work serenely without physical problems that would affect your own work.

Each and every one has its own trading style, and as you have this you will also have preferences on how to get comfortable so you can concentrate on work and investments.

How to start Swing Trading from home

Many people who enter the world of swing trading either come from jobs that no longer satisfied him, or were fired and forced to reinvent themselves, there are also people who simply have the desire to build something beyond the constraints of a salary fixed.

Becoming an investment instructor and entrepreneur appears to be an interesting path for them.

Many people who have walked this path today advise how to take this path.

If you are unfamiliar, swing trading is a method of capitalizing on the movement of shares in a short time, unlike day trading in which trading is much shorter and occurs with the market open and closed.

If you are a beginner, swing trading is a much more accessible practice that is also less stressful.

Through personal discipline and daily practice, it's something you can do anytime, from anywhere and once you understand the mechanism, it's easy to make money.

How to get started? The best advice I can give you is this:

Position yourself as a student.

One of the mistakes that cost the most (to your portfolio) is what new traders may not be able to invest in.

Like everything new, just known, it takes time to understand the internal functioning of the market, you also need it to interpret the movements of the market or how news influences it and still how to find your personal style.

And after the first tip, I want to provide you with others that will come in handy during this trading experience:

> *Subscribe to platforms that send a trading email newsletter*

> *Download an app that allows you to operate*

> *Take an online course*

> *Always watch others trade and listen to the reasons behind the decisions they make*

On these points we need to broaden the discussion by asking ourselves a question, namely: between research and comments who is saying what?

It takes method and discipline to understand what to select from the avalanche of information that you will receive during this work "adventure".

Earn with the money you have already accumulated

When you start swing trading, you often have a lot of debt.

So it becomes stressful to go find the best way to invest in the stock market.

So reinvesting the money earned is a way to protect yourself from further debt situations.

If you don't, you are playing on a very soft track.

If you don't have a lot of money to reinvest, it's okay. You can start simply by learning more about the practice.

So study, study a lot and select the best tips.

Before investing money, engage in practice and invest in your education and training. Only then will you see if you are truly a trader.

Once you are ready to put some more money into these investments, you can enjoy penny stocks (stocks under $ 10) or take a few thousand dollars (at least 2,000) and start trading.

This approach is certainly more risky due to the fact that with a small amount of money to invest, you do not have the privilege of distributing it on a series of choices.

If you really want to participate in this business, a base sum of 8500 euros represents an all-in sum of money to be exchanged.

This amount allows you to distribute enough money on a number of varied choices to protect you from losing your entire account.

Small victories in the choices made can quickly constitute a portfolio that lasts over time.

Going to conclude on this point it must be said that if you still cannot make money with money, you are not prepared to start operating in swing trading.

Have an operational plan and constantly stick to it

Once you have started learning techniques by accumulating information on the swing trading process and are ready to make your first investment, it is essential to have an operational plan on how to get in and out of the different trades.

Keep in mind that there is no perfect practice or perfect exit.

Having this truth at your disposal always tries to achieve returns of 5-10 percent.

In this way, you can be reassured that the right supplies are being collected as you move forward.

It is logical that in order to have a good operational plan available, we rely on knowledge of stocks and constant practice.

That's why it's important to spend some time trading with fake securities, for example on an app, using fake money before putting your hard-earned money into this business practice.

Swing trading can become your next successful business or a way to earn extra income, retirement plans, or to be able to make big purchases like a house.

Swing Trading, the complete definition

The English word Swing takes on the meaning of swing.

Swing Trading is a trading style that is mainly used in medium and long term time horizons.

The purpose of this approach is to take advantage of market movements or fluctuations by going for open transactions for several days or weeks.

A Swing Trading position remains open for more than a day, some can last up to several weeks.

The trader usually performs his analysis on a daily chart, or using a 4-hour chart.

He spends only a few minutes every day looking for trading opportunities, for the rest of the time he tends to let his scenarios evolve on their own, this is the crucial point in Swing Trading.

This trading style is applicable to all CFD instruments on:

> *actions,*

> *raw material,*

> *stock market indices.*

> *Forex.*

If you are looking out for this type of trading only now, for the first time, I recommend you practice some free demo accounts that you can easily find online.

But in swing trading what are the forex strategies you can adopt?

Swing trading has analogies with the trend trading distributed over the long term, but the market movements are still slower.

This is the reason why the trader swing always looks for graphic models of several days and tries to obtain movements or price changes that are higher than those usually obtained in daily transactions.

A swing trader can employ a combination of fundamental analysis and technical analysis to accompany his decisions.

It does not matter if there is a long-term trend or if the market is largely tied to a range. A swing trader will not hold a position too long to count representatively.

Volatility is the keystone for Swing Traders.

The more volatile the market appears (and claims) and the more price movements in the short term are generated, the more opportunities are created to open a Swing operation.

The advantages of Forex swing trading

Swing Trading is an extremely suitable method for the Forex market for various reasons:

- ➢ *It has many similarities to the classic investment you can make in the stock market.*

- ➢ *You can trade on a weekly, monthly or yearly trend.*

- ➢ *The Forex market is a market with high liquidity and volatility, this characteristic increases the opportunities for price movements in a rather short period of time.*

As we have already pointed out, short-term trading requires constant monitoring.

As seen, on the other hand, long-term trading may also not be sufficiently dynamic and active.

This is the reason why the time horizon of Swing Trading makes this type of trading truly captivating and attractive, especially if you are a beginner.

But what about the Spread?

In this field of action, reality tells us that for a swing trader the spread does not have much relevance because this trader goes on very large time scales that a spread of a few points or pips is not perceived as a disadvantage.

At this point I want to give you 10 tips or steps to do Swing Trading with good results.

I'll show them to you in the numbered list:

- *Take on losses and let profits run*
- *Swing Trading and Discipline, the solution is to have patience*
- *Buy in support areas and sell in resistance areas*
- *Go to operate in line with the general trend*
- *Wait for the demotion to be confirmed to enter the market at the best levels*
- *Buy cheap and sell dearly*
- *Open the position at the right time*
- *Monitor your losses constantly*
- *Always try to have a profit target and a loss limit in trading before going to occupy a position in the market*
- *Constantly analyzes the markets through technical analyzes.*

There are obviously guidelines that you will have to follow scrupulously.

For example, remember that swing trading is a trading style and not a strategy in itself.

Many indicators, even very different from each other, may be suitable for this style of trading, in particular any method that tends to detect the trend and that can concretely help you to trade on the trend.

But at this point I have to give you an example to understand the different scenarios in terms of price and risk.

Keep in mind that it may be necessary to study many charts before deciding which method best suits your personal trader profile.

Swing Trading strategies and how to make money on the stock market with this tool

Have you ever wondered what happens if you can't close the deal on time?

There can always be unexpected price bounces.

For this reason, good risk management must always be adopted and price action monitored.

I'll give you an example.

In the early hours of June 24, 2016, the results of Brexit's vote began to be evident.

What was the impact on the stock market?

The one for which the pound's value plummeted.

If a trader had kept his position he would have been trapped in a bad operation for a long time.

With the announcement of Brexit, a drop of several hundred pips occurred in a small time, it is estimated less than a minute.

In such circumstances, good risk management is essential.

If your position is the right size with respect to your capital and your risk management, you will be able to withstand unexpected episodes like the one that happened in 2016. But let's see how you can resist going into detail.

But what are the best Swing Trading strategies and how to manage risk?

A key aspect of swing trading is the ability to be and remain profitable. In other words, this aspect is related to the optimal management of your investment.

But what is the best management of your investment when you operate in swing trading?

Risk or investment management or "money management" is nothing more than the administration and management of money that is dedicated to trading.

In trading, but particularly in Forex, you need to know how to lose before knowing how to win. And when it comes to learning how to lose, I mean that you need to know how to take on small losses in order to win more.

The Swing Trading Forex strategy with risk management involves careful money management.

To explain this principle in substance, two aspects need to be considered.

> *How willing you are to lose*

> *What is your panic threshold*

Below we will talk about money management in Swing Trading to answer these questions and establish a global strategy.

Instead, the second aspect to consider is what you need to know how to automate risk management in Swing Trading - or any other type of Trading - and, at the same time, ensure some flexibility.

If the markets are optimistic, you will be willing to take more risks. You will be referred to as top of the range in money management, while in a bear market, you will probably be less certain and prefer to take less risk.

The trader profile you want to have

The first thing to do when you start trading is to know the risk aversion and volatility of the different markets you will be working on.

In other words, at what stage of the loss you will begin to be afraid.

I strongly advise you not to act as if you are not afraid, well people are taught to be weak to say or think they are afraid but fear is an irrepressible human instinct, so it is impossible not to have it, and if you don't calculate it, it will be you to manage you, instead of you to manage it.

I will give you an effective example based on a share (if any) of capital that you will manage. Let's say you have € 20,000 capital at your disposal and you lose € 2,000, then will you have lost 10% of your capital, will your world collapse or will you experience it as something you were mentally prepared for?

The answer to this question depends on trader to trader so you have to rely on yourself.

In summary, to understand and orient yourself, (also because you can also think of bearing certain losses but then be alarmed in front of them) you must take into account some personal factors:

> *your past experiences,*

> *how did you experience youth,*

> *your parents and what they educated you to do,*

> *what did you take from the wider social sphere (outside the family that affects you most),*

> *financial education.*

With this example I wanted to show you a simple factor, namely that we are not all the same and that this will define our aversion to risk and volatility.

All this set of characteristics inherent in trading is called "Investor Profile".

Where the psychological aspect of the stock market reveals parts of yourself that you may not know or have not paid due attention to.

Another question you can ask yourself to test your fear is the following:

would you administer 10% of your investment in the same way if it was 20,000 euros and if it was 200,000 euros?

Understanding risk management in Swing Trading is very important (as you will have understood by now).

One thing you should be clear about in the forex or stock market is that you won't win every time you trade. In some trades profits will be made and losses will accumulate in others. It would be wrong to think that you can only ever get a profit. The sooner you assume and understand this scenario, the better it is for yourself and to operate!

Another point that assumes some importance, so that you will have to consider is to be able to quickly exit an operation when the market collapses.

Note that I wrote "when" and not "if", because the market will certainly collapse. And for the second time, the sooner you calculate it and get a reason for it, the better!

In fact, the flexibility that you get if the market changes allows you to sell very quickly, which is important for small traders.

Large institutions cannot "escape" from the mechanisms that the market constantly puts before them. And this is a trap that they themselves have put in place.

It is not a pessimistic view at all, but on the contrary it is realistic. At regular intervals since the beginning of the 19th century, markets collapse, the capitalist system collapses and this will happen again, in a cyclical way.

But until this happens, we will learn to manage our money in the strategy that Swing Trading prepares.

Find out much more about risk management and trading in general through the free training materials that you can find online and that I also want to introduce you today.

The daily management of investments with a Swing Trading Strategy, for example, will involve a series of rules that you will have to learn in the short term and then you will have to be ready to apply them.

Once you understand what the big picture is, you still need to manage the risk you face every day.

The question is:

How to manage your capital daily?

It is actually quite simple, although it may seem complex if you are a beginner in the field.

If you want to keep an overall risk of 6% just to give you an example, consider protecting 6 "non-neutralized" operations, that is 6 times the 1% of your monetary investment.

It is understood that you will be authorized to lose 1% of your capital in 6 different operations or a maximum of 200 euros per single transaction if your investment starts from a share of 20,000 euros.

The technique you choose for the daily management of your investment will best understand it when you start trading.

But what must be clear a priori is that you can come to 6 operations and that your risk will not go beyond what you have planned.

Then, before taking a position, it is necessary to be aware that the maximum risk for a correct management of the capital in Swing Trading must be (based on the example I have given you) of 1% or equal to 200 euros.

Therefore, your stop-loss and neutralization position will be determined before each trade. And from there you will have to try to get as much as possible without going beyond risk management.

Only this you need to know! I said it was not complex, of course practice is needed.

And in the meantime, your actions are evolving. In simple terms, it is sold so that the result of the operation is that of reaching the loss limit.

Or you stop trading so that the asset goes up and reaches free Trading, basically it turns and sells in its initial purchase area and nothing is lost.

Therefore, if one of your 6 "confirmed" transactions becomes free, you can take a new position, without daring beyond your risk limit.

Financial products for Swing Trading

The swing trading activities can be currencies such as EURUSD, futures, cfds on the dax 30, cryptocurrencies and in general assets that have a certain volatility.

Let's take a closer look at swing trading strategies to highlight the risk and reward factors manifested in operations.

To begin with, simple strategies are needed to develop other more complex versions, based on different types of analysis, but above all on a coherent technical analysis of the financial markets.

N ° 1: The Swing Trading Forex strategies

Before starting with any theory or practice, it is essential to know that swing trading is a style or type of trading, not a strategy in and of itself.

The time frame is the variable that defines the style or type of trading. Each type of trading involves numerous strategies that can be learned and used.

The trading strategies that I report below do not exclusively concern Swing Trading.

These concepts give you two options in your swing trading strategy:

> *Follow the trend.*

> *Trade on it.*

Antitrend strategies go to seek profit when maintaining support and resistance levels.

On the other hand, trend following strategies look for those moments when support and resistance levels are interrupted.

For each of the two types it is very useful to have the ability to visually recognize the action that the price is about to perform.

A short note on the price action should be made:

Markets never move in a straight line, even when at the last minute the trend is bullish or bearish in staggered movements.

There is an upward trend from the market that sets higher highs, and a downward trend with lower lows.

Many swing trading strategies consist of trying to find and follow a short trend, but it is also necessary to take a look at counter-trend exchanges.

No. 2: Swing Trading Strategies - How long does a pullback last?

Here is another aspect to consider.

We have no way of knowing how long a pullback will last. Instead, it is necessary to seek confirmation that the market has resumed its native trend.

In other words, if you trade you will:

> *Look for a trend*

> *Looking forward to a trend change*

You will enter the market after seeing that the trend change has ended and the trend has stabilized again.

The telltale sign you are looking for is a recovery in the market by setting higher highs.

At this point it has been understood that the market sets ever higher peaks: and it is equally important to be aware of the fact that even the lows have increased over each period.

N ° 3: Swing Trading Strategy - Why not employ a take profit?

You don't take a take profit if you want to let your profits last as long as possible.

It is not possible to know (in advance) how long the trend will last, nor is it possible to know the maximums that will be reached.

Avoid making predictions knowing this by setting a price target.

However, you can know that prices do not go up in a short time.

This means that you will have to allow the market to move to some extent in a negative way, and then continue the trend.

It also means that when the trend stops, you will have to return part of the profits before closing orders.

N ° 4: Swing Trading Strategy in countertrend

Our third strategy aims to tend to carry out a countertrend operation, and therefore operates in opposition to the previously viewed strategies.

Try to spot the short-term trend.

At this point you will try to benefit from the frequency with which this trend tends to break.

Remember that, as indicated above:

> ➢ *Rising highs suggest an upward trend,*

> ➢ *Declining lows suggest a bearish trend.*

It has been seen that the beginning of a trend can be followed by a period of reversal before the trend resumes.

A trader who works against the trend can also try to take advantage of the swing in the return period.

To do this you will try to recognize the upward trend model.

Then when a new high is followed by a sequence of failures to break new highs you will go to position in short in anticipation of the change.

Once you go against the trend, it is very important to maintain strong discipline if the price moves against us.

If the market resumes its tendency against the position you have taken, you must keep yourself ready to admit that you have made a mistake and accept and take on the losses.

All the strategies examined so far are simple. They count on your ability to recognize and understand the price action.

Other operations you can carry out to optimize your Swing Trading strategy?

In reality, the ways you can optimize your strategy are many and different from each other.

The first is to make your business coincide with the long-term trend.

N ° 1: Try to trade only when your direction matches what you are seeing in the long term trend.

Another way to improve your strategy is to use a secondary technical indicator to confirm what you are working on in your theories.

To give you an example:

If you are a trader who works against the trend and you are thinking of selling, you will constantly monitor the RSI to make sure it signals the hyper-bought market.

Moving average (MA) is another indicator that you can use to help yourself. A moving average softens prices to give a clearer view of the trend.

And since the moving average encompasses the old data prices, this represents an easy way to compare the current price by comparing it with previous prices.

Latest Tips for Swing Forex Trading

If you operate on a large portfolio of currency pairs you will need to analyze as many currency pairs as possible to find the best trading opportunities and the tool that best suits your swing trader characteristics.

The Forex market constantly guarantees you trading opportunities, so it is you who must look for the ones that best suit your way of trading.

> ➢ *Keep track of swaps*

the value of the swap must be taken seriously in swing trading, always keeping in mind that the latter can be both positive and negative.

As an example, starting from September 9, 2019, the swaps of Admiral Markets on the Euro Dollar are:

> *1,315 for long SWAP positions, is the amount that will be subtracted from a long position from the daily financial costs.*

> *+0.339 for SWAP in short positions, this is the amount that will be added to a short position by the daily financial costs.*

You can't forget that no commissions are charged at the entry or exit of your trade.

The permanence of positive profit-loss ratios: whether it is H4 or daily charts, in swing trading you can take advantage of large market movements, having the opportunity to obtain a higher profit ratio than possible losses in a scalping strategy.

> *Put your emotions aside, or better, manage them so that they don't get in the way of your strategy*

it is better not to trade by letting go of the emotions, but it is necessary to open the trades as part of a currency trading plan and a strengthened strategy, in a clear, planned and organized way.

> *Follow the trend*

swing trading is much easier to manage by following the trend rather than through countertrend trading.

To conclude and after showing you some entry and exit strategies for swing trading, I tell you that it is important to keep in mind that a complete forex swing trading system must also include good money management and an accurate identification of the most adequate markets.

Other good practices you can implement are as follows:

> *Avoid trading against the general trend of the market.*

> *Use a second indicator to confirm the signal of the first indicator.*

> *Have a clear idea of your exit threshold and keep it below the profits you have decided on.*

> *Test your strategies in an environment that does not present risks with our demo account, before starting to trade with a real account.*

Remaining always on the theme of how Swing Trading works, it must be said that in order to make swing trading profitable, it is necessary to select a market that is in a very precise directional trend, be it bullish or bearish.

When prices temporarily deviate from the main trend you can operate by aiming for a return of prices close to the trend itself.

You will have to avoid the lateral market phases those defined as trading range or consolidation since they can lead to errors and cause heavy losses.

Precisely in order to avoid running into this error, traders often use indicators to see if the market is trending or not.

Among these indicators, the best known is the simple (or exponential) moving average.

Going into detail, if the moving average crosses the price line downwards and has a positive inclination, the market is rising.

On the contrary, if the moving average crosses the price line upwards and has a negative inclination, then the market presents itself in a bearish trend.

There are many other indicators that can tell you if a market is trending or not.

It should also be borne in mind that many operators prefer to use a greater number of indicators at the same time in order to increase the effectiveness of swing trading, reducing the possibility of incurring false signals.

The advantages that swing trading can offer you are many.

The main advantage of this trading technique is provided by the time horizon you will be working on.

This has meant that this modus operandi has spread over the years, going beyond the limits related to both intraday operations and those related to buy & hold.

Staying on intraday operations, it must be said that investors (defined as scalpers) risk limiting potential profits, when they close their position during the day (sometimes even just a few minutes!) And not taking advantage of the trend that is revealed.

Furthermore, operating intraday involves having more time and often a high level of stress.

In such a general picture, it is easy to get overwhelmed by emotions, risking to further aggravate losses.

And then there are the operating limits of the buy & hold.

If intraday operations have limits, we cannot say that the buy & hold strategy is immune to them.

In this case the main risk is that the positions are left open for too long, for example many months, with profits that can be quickly eroded if the market suddenly changes its course.

In addition, many traders consider this operating technique uninteresting, given that operations are reduced to a few operations per month.

**However, the advantages of swing trading are there! Even if reading what I have just reported you may feel no longer attracted to this world, it is always necessary to balance not only the risks but also the intentions.**

Swing trading overcomes all these obstacles that you can face.

In the first instance, trading is not as hectic and stressful as in intraday trading and, at the same time, it is not as bland as in buy & hold.

In the second instance, through swing trading, traders let any profits run, taking advantage of the bullish or bearish movement of the market in the short term, without having to close the operation early.

In any case, discipline must always be used when operating on the financial markets.

For this reason, even with swing trading it is always recommended to use risk management techniques, such as stop losses and price targets.

Swing trading is adaptable to any asset, including:

- ➤ *actions,*
- ➤ *indices,*
- ➤ *forex,*
- ➤ *commodity,*

even if its maximum diffusion is in the currency market.

The high volatility and liquidity that circulate daily on this market allow operators to make good profits even in a multi day time frame, unlike indices and commodities where volatility can sometimes be very contained for long periods of time.

Definition of Green Business: everything you need to know

The definition of a green company concerns a company that has no negative impact on the environment, economy or community.

This type of company sets the horizon of foresight when it comes to issues such as:

> *human rights,*

> *environmental concerns*

> *all issues related to the first two points.*

Green enterprises are going to use environmentally sustainable resources and respect socially responsible policies.

Routing a green business is not complex, what is missing is a general idea of what we are policies and green economies, in some countries these policies are in fact very fragmented.

If you are a small entrepreneur who wants to transform his business by making it sustainable, you will have to implement best practices that lead you to zero impact or in any case to reduce it as much as possible.

Such as?

I start from the purchases you have to make.

when it comes to topics such as shopping, but also:

> *product development,*

> *production,*

> *supply of products*

> *supply of services.*

Environmental responsibility becomes the main feature that puts a clear separation between green companies and those that do not take into account their impact on the environment.

Many think (and it is a preconception also quite widespread unfortunately) that only small businesses can implement an ecological conversion, instead there are many companies of all sizes that have chosen to become green.

They range from sole proprietorships to Fortune 500 companies.

Ecological strategies not only preserve and take care of natural resources, but can also reduce costs and improve efficiency.

When choosing the green road, consider four basic areas:

- ➤ *Reduction of energy consumption and improvement of energy efficiency.*
- ➤ *Elimination of waste and use of sustainable materials.*
- ➤ *Adherence to environmental regulations and good practices.*
- ➤ *Purchase of ecological equipment, products and services.*

Within each of these practices, changes can be made ranging from basic improvements to more complex and far-reaching projects.

But what is (in fact) sustainability?

The concept of sustainability has three key elements:

- ➤ *the social element,*
- ➤ *the economic element,*
- ➤ *the environmental element.*

Each of these asks those who open a small, medium or large company to adopt measures that meet the needs of their company while preserving resources for future generations.

Environmental stability affects several resources, including:

- ➤ *water,*
- ➤ *waste management system,*
- ➤ *power,*
- ➤ *emissions,*
- ➤ *natural resources.*

Businesses are considered 100% sustainable if they replace the resources they employ, while unsustainable businesses cause excess pollution and use more resources than they can replace.

Economic sustainability is about a company that is making a profit instead of getting into debt.

This category therefore also includes the purchase of products that reduce the environmental impact, an example are energy-efficient appliances.

Social sustainability (which intersects with environmental sustainability) concerns the way in which a society returns to its community:

- ➤ **Ethical principles,**

- ➢ *instruction,*
- ➢ *Charity programs,*
- ➢ *human rights provisions,*
- ➢ *health and safety measures,*
- ➢ *opportunity,*
- ➢ *fair wages,*
- ➢ *extended quality of life for employees.*

All these practices also include activities to combat unethical behavior and the guarantee that the supply and resource chain is free of human rights violations.

When it comes to becoming green and if you are an entrepreneur, the question of environmental sustainability does not allow shadows, I explain myself in simple and direct words:

- ➢ *Or are you Green*
- ➢ *Or you're not Green*

This does not mean that you have to blame yourself if you can only achieve certain goals, but that you have to consider them all from the beginning to understand how far you are willing to go.

Basically to decide how far you want to go, consider a few questions:

- ➢ *Why do I want to become sustainable?*
- ➢ *What market factors should I consider?*
- ➢ *How can becoming environmentally and socially sustainable give me an edge over the competition?*
- ➢ *How does the green fit my business plan?*
- ➢ *What aspects of green business do I want to adopt?*
- ➢ *• How can I get a competitive advantage in areas where I don't want to go green?*
- ➢ *• Are there groups and resources for green businesses in my sector or in my area?*
- ➢ *• What steps will I take to make sure that the products and services I purchase are green?*

One of the most relevant aspects when it comes to the green economy is that which relates to the carbon footprint that your company has and therefore that of its environmental impact in terms of carbon dioxide produced by a specific activity.

If you cannot or do not want to reduce the action that carbon plays in your company, you can take steps to reduce its impact.

This could include purchasing carbon credits from an ethical company to compensate for the carbon dioxide employed by your company.

Do you know the so-called "Green Business Certification"?

Many organizations can provide certification for ecological business standards and sustainability measures.

But let's see what are the most common requirements of these certification programs that include:

➢ *Adoption of measures to prevent pollution and reduce waste*

➢ *An accurate management of hazardous materials and chemicals*

➢ *Ensure consumer and employee education programs on sustainability*

➢ *Conservation of natural resources*

➢ *Respect for environmental laws*

When you decide to switch to an ecological economy model, use the local resources designed to help you succeed.

You may be looking for a tutor in another company in your industry that has successfully implemented sustainability measures.

You can also access resources, training and tools that are set up by government agencies if available.

Some small steps you can take to reduce the environmental impact include small steps, really simple choices that you can implement at any time although they seem very expensive for personal energy are not complex to implement:

➢ *Eliminate the plastic bottles*

➢ *Switch to energy saving LED bulbs*

➢ *Working with vendors and suppliers who carry out and implement sustainable practices*

➢ *Use cleaning products that do not use polluting components*

Below I want to offer you an introduction to the green economy.

How can we deal with interconnected economic and environmental crises in the world?

Many people speak of the green economy as a solution, but not everyone agrees.

So the question is, "Why choose the Green Economy?"

That of the green economy is the point that brings together the ideas of the global North and South on economy, energy, environment and climate change while thinking about moving towards a more sustainable model on a planet whose resources have been abused.

The idea of a more sustainable economy has been debated for decades.

A key moment in this discussion was the publication of the Limits to Growth report produced by the Club of Rome in 1972.

So almost 50 years ago.

In recent years, the discussion on sustainability has become a key part of the global agenda.

This happened because the latest scientific studies and our direct experiences of environmental devastation and climate change are making it clear that the economic model is changing.

The green economy was the central theme of the great United Nations conference on sustainable development (Rio + 20) held in Rio in June 2012.

It is therefore necessary to observe what the chronology of the decisions taken on the green economy has been from the beginning to today.

Our growing understanding of the extent of environmental degradation and climate change brought by anthropocentrism have pushed forward the idea of a green economy, putting it on the top of the global agenda in recent years.

There have been some key events of the last few decades, I will show them on the list below.

> *Rio1972 Summit Stockholm Conference*

> *1987 Brundtland report*

> *1992 Earth Summit and Agenda 21*

> *Rio + 20 2012 conference*

But a question that few people ask (and instead is the right question to ask) is: Why is there a debate about what the green economy is?

The demand is not so obvious, because under the word "green" methods and practices that had little to do with sustainability have also been included!

The green economy means different things to different people.

Sometimes these perspectives overlap and others contradict each other.

Some people reject the concept of a green economy.

Back: Why Green Economy? is to present these different points of view so that a general assessment can be made.

The following examples illustrate only two perspectives on the green economy, but they are particular and you will soon understand why:

> ## N ° 1: The United Nations Environment Program (defined with the UNEP acronym)

The key reference point for most of the work related to the green economy comes from the United Nations Environment Program (UNEP) and reads the following:

"A green economy is one that translates into an improvement in human well-being and social equity, while significantly reducing environmental risks and ecological shortages. In its simplest expression, a green economy can be thought of as a low carbon, resource efficient and socially inclusive economy.
"

This is only a summary of the UNEP Green Economy Report, but if you understand the political push from this, the second position is the one I illustrate below.

> ## No. 2: Creative Common Goods not a green economy

The concept of common goods is not about politics detached from reality, it is about the people and civil society movements that held an alternative summit during the United Nations conference on sustainable development Rio + 20 in June 2012, this group concluded that :

"The so-called 'green economy is just another aspect of the current financial phase of capitalism, which also uses old and new mechanisms, such as the deepening of public-private debt, the hyperstimulation of consumption, the concentration of ownership of new technologies , the carbon and biodiversity markets, land grabbing, the increase in foreign land ownership and public-private partnerships, among others. "

In essence, there are various social actors who claim that the green economy represents their point of view.

This led to confusion about how to define the green economy and to some groups that totally reject the concept.

It is necessary to identify which are the key areas of the debate.

- Current debates on how to measure growth and prosperity will have important consequences for global trade, production and consumption patterns.

- On the subject of Energy: The energy sources that we will use in the future will be fundamental for the functioning of our societies and economies.

- Valorization of nature: any idea related to the recognition of the true value of nature (monetary and / or non-monetary) can tangire on the way in which we protect the environment, safeguarding it for future generations.

Is monitoring methods and places also a method?

Again ethical conflicts arise.

When monitoring is aimed at respecting the environment, should it be considered control?

The topic is thorny, but maps, tools and infographics are now widely spread, also by virtue of the fact that technology has made gigantic steps in this direction, however posing an ethical question, that related to how to find information, how and how much to find it. without being invasive on one aspect, that of the balance and privacy of areas and people.

How can the green economy find relevance for your job?

The green economy brings together a large area of policy and research.

Many of the issues related to this social and economic approach are related to possible domino effects.

Below I want to report some potential impacts on the different thematic areas:

- Development model

Putting a model of development in the North and South of the world that has an increasing weight in the economic sectors based on energy and the environment (eg natural capital) at the center of the discussion is important, and provides a global vision rather than a narrow and often very selfish view.

Strong links between nature conservation and poverty reduction are associated to bring a new model.

- Some aid promotes a green economy.

More information on: objectives of the green economy poverty and inequality Rio + 20, the theme of poverty is not necessarily disconnected from a green economy, so much so that many populations find alone solutions suitable for environmental sustainability, solutions as simple as effective.

> *Green growth after 2015 MDG and SDG beyond growth and GDP (analysis)*

Ideas related to the enhancement of nature could have a huge impact on how the environment is preserved.

New economic sectors that focus their attention on the environment could change our approach to nature (examples are the Bioeconomy, and the so-called natural capital).

> *Energy*

The transition from fossil fuels to renewable energies is at the heart of all the talk about a green economy.

The energy sources that are used globally (whether they are fossil fuels or renewable sources) will determine our ability to avoid climate change which we now know is irreversible.

The insights are important on climate change, fossil fuels and renewable energy, that's why I want to discuss them starting from a related topic which is this:

> *Conflict & Security*

Climate change has already impacted on existing conflicts and is creating new ones.

The security issue has also become strategic.

Suffice it to note in particular the case relating to local communities that are geographically located in what has been defined as the global south, and their access to resources.

The potential conflicts that will arise in the future (because it will happen that will occur) being connected to the green economy within or among local communities could arise from:

> - *Climate mitigation projects (perhaps with an increase in land use and private property conflicts)*

> - *Climate reworking projects (such as the disparity in the distribution of aid)*

> - *Projects related to natural capital (such as conservation which actually limits the means of subsistence)*

> - *Control and location suitable for energy projects (such as large-scale dams)*

International newspapers and "Green" positions

BLOOMBERG recently wrote an article where he highlights how the Corona Virus (Covid-19) can be caught as a stimulus for a change that is truly such.

The title of the article is:

"A green stimulus plan for a post-coronavirus economy"

It is highlighted as a group consisting of:

> - *economists,*

> - *academics,*

> - *politicians (USA)*

You argue that the Covid-19 pandemic can be read as an opportunity to remedy the economic crisis by looking at the earth with other eyes and doing it with a long-term perspective.

If in this period the emergency phase of this pandemic is disappearing, the proposal of these experts is to get out of it with an economic, environmental, social and political "revolution" by subverting the status quo.

In essence, the message left by this group of US economists, professors and veterans relating to the latest financial crisis was collected and took the form of a letter sent to Congress asking that it legislate starting from 'green stimuli' aimed at restarting the economy in order to regulate and control climate change and poverty.

The request is equal to $ 2 trillion dollars that go to develop programs capable of creating:

- jobs,

- areas for public health,

- extended housing and a center far from an energy structure based on fossil fuels.

According to the plan elaborated by these professional figures, the stimulus will automatically renew itself every year for 4% of GDP, therefore with $ 850 billion per year.

But this elaboration sent to a man who until yesterday has denied the existence of climate change does not stop there.

It is asked to provide people with more say on how and how large companies can access public bailouts.

For now, this group recognizes that attention should focus on stopping the spread of coronavirus and mitigating all related health risks.

Legislative action and planning work according to the movement spokesman:

'They can ensure that physical projects start as soon as the situation makes it possible by restarting work across the economy.'

The US Congress is already preparing a bill for economic recovery, to help workers recover income and businesses and governments to recover lost revenue from the coronavirus pandemic.

But the United States Senate is currently stalled over a debate (which seems endless) and exists between those Republicans who want to dedicate a quarter of the $ 1.8 trillion stimulus plan to give money only to companies without reference to any environment and an economy that is not selfish.

Instead, the Democrats intend to ensure rigorous transparency and take control of how the $ 500 billion corporate bailouts will be recorded.

Democrats are also pursuing their demands, one of which is that of airlines receiving federal financial assistance by asking that they agree to cut carbon emissions by 50% and that companies pay a minimum wage of $ 15 to workers.

The "green" will proposes to Congress to give greater impetus to ensuring that workers are protected and that companies have the opportunity to operate in a sustainable way to avoid the catastrophes of climate change, especially in an economy paralyzed by the coronavirus.

The authors of the proposal focus on a broad-based recovery, a theme to be added to the stimulus of the American Recovery and Reinvestment Act of 2009 (we are always in the States) approvato dall'amministrazione Obama e che è giunto dopo il piano di salvataggio dell'Emergency Economic Stabilization Act 2008 administration Bush.

Indeed, many of the authors of the letter focused on the green economy have worked on the 2009 ARRA legislation or are currently working on legislative proposals related to a green New Deal, and in some of them deal with both issues.

It must be said that much of the Green Stimulus package reflects the green New Deal.

The BLOOMBERG article cites the architects of Green Stimulus highlighting how they are operating taking into account the guidelines established by a coalition of climate and environmental justice organizations that define themselves as: "Five Principles for Just Covid-19 Relief and Stimulus ".

They focus on certain issues (ethical but also economic):

➢ *public health.*

➢ *direct economic aid to families,*

➢ *lighten workers instead of company managers,*

➢ *protection of elections and all democratic processes,*

➢ *create an 'advance on a regenerative economy'.*

The last principle is what the "green" stimulus seeks to pursue.

'As politicians take steps to ensure immediate relief and long-term recovery, it is imperative to take into consideration the related crises of wealth inequality, racism and ecological decline, which were taking place long before Covid-19 and which now they are likely to intensify, '

This is what the principles indicate.

CityLab magazine interviewed J. Mijin Cha, author of Green Stimulus, senior fellow at Data for Progress and assistant professor of urban and environmental policy at Western College.

A large part of his scholarship dedicated it to the theme of the transition to a low carbon economy and to the system designed to prepare workers in the fossil fuel sector and the unemployed to enter the world of renewable energy.

The interview carried out gives us a glimpse of how the study is also contributing to an objective need and this interview has been very accurate both for the clarity it expresses and for the length.

Why focus on a transition that represents equity for workers?

Not only because of a moral issue that still weighs given the economic crisis, but also because the transition from companies that use fossil fuels to reach converted companies or started from renewable energy, the important issue to talk about in the midst of a coronavirus pandemic is precisely that of the potential that this period despite the health and painful situation presents.

There is also a situation (which is still an emergency) that communities that are struggling with coronavirus find themselves without the resources to fight it properly, and certain rural regions still depend almost entirely on fossil fuels.

If we think about the stimulus that the Green Economy offers, this push also concerns workers who should be an active part of the change itself. Also because putting an end to the extraction of fossil fuels tomorrow is not something that is considered feasible by this manager.

According to J. Mijin Cha, it takes at least 10 years to better plan economic diversification and implement it so that these communities do not move from a tax base linked to coal mines to nothing.

This is just one opinion among the others, however, and it is an opinion that extends the extraction of fossil fuels for another 10 years since it takes this time to develop a plan, so it allows this time to pass and since the alternative is nothing it is understood that for another 10 years, according to this approach, it is invited to continue polluting.

However, we understand how essential it is to work to move communities from fossil fuels to something that needs to be implemented now.

From a health point of view, renewable energies obviously protect workers more while we know perfectly well that extracting fossil fuels poses high health risks.

The health impacts of these extractive industries seem to make people more sensitive to viruses like covid-19 if they are not healthy.

There are also several provisions that focus on investments in women for a recovery that also takes into account this aspect which is particularly sensitive in every area of the world. Why is it relevant?

If you look at the statistics on the occupations most affected by this pandemic, you can see how these are:

> *health care*

> *education*

And who works most in these two areas?

Women.

We can say that women will suffer the greatest weight of the negative economic consequences that emerge in the post coronavirus recovery.

This emphasis on women is not a truth but also a way to recognize that historically women have been excluded from things, production and technology have organized themselves by polluting and precisely excluding, therefore with a social model that was in bankruptcy, but which today proves even more that it is.

In this discussion and unraveling clear data it is necessary to turn our gaze towards low-income communities, African communities, indigenous communities and other frontline communities that have historically been excluded both from the extractive economy and from the current neoliberal economy that we are experiencing now.

The data on women speaks of something wider, it is true that women are still treated as a minority in need of protection at work, a green economy must be an inclusive economy, not based on quotas, which does not exclude peoples (such as those above highlighted) that does not provide for sexual hierarchies, nor other types of vertical ladders.

Currently there is a large bibliography dedicated to green conversion, a bibliography that takes into consideration different political positions, and not all agree with the approach highlighted above, indeed some would like to apply the same exclusions that have been made so far, without criticizing the social model but only the environmental one.

But the two issues cannot be considered separately, for a variety of reasons.

The current state of the green economy in Italy and in the world is highly fragmented, investigations have been conducted on the topic that highlight this fragmentation.

The Report and the proposals of the General States of the green economy 2018 by Toni Federico, Foundation for sustainable development give us a glimpse of Italy and the rest of the world.

Here are the data that emerged for Italy in 2017:

> *1st among the great European countries in circular economy,*

> *1st in organic farming*

> *1st in eco-innovation*

But those shown above are only the positive data, very negative is instead (as suggested by the image that does not concern Italy but which says how abusing the soil can lead to catastrophic consequences) the data on the so-called land consumption.

Other negative data concern:

> *the protection of biodiversity*

> *decarbonisation.*

The state of the transition to the green economy in Italy and in the world is analyzed in the traditional "Report on the state of the green economy 2018" which was presented in November on the inaugural day of the General States of the green economy at Ecomondo.

On a global level (given that it is on this that the capitalist chessboard plays its game and for which it is this plan that must be considered) the green economy was at the center of the final day of the General States, with a comparison between international actors, institutions and industry on a particularly important topic:

"Italy is not in the zero year in the green economy," said Sergio Costa, Minister of the Environment and of the protection of the territory and the sea, on that occasion.

"Investing in green economy means doing circular economy and the circular economy must replace the linear economy because resources are not unlimited. The economic benefits of these green investments are manifold ".

Edo Ronchi, then President of the Foundation for Sustainable Development, argued that:

"The first concerns the avoided costs of pollution and other environmental impacts; the second the ability of these green choices to activate, with public investments, multiplier effects also of private ones; the third advantage lies in the ability to use and promote innovation, dissemination of good practices and good techniques ".

As work continued, the results of the international analysis on the state of the green economy were summarized, which the Report examines by giving priority to the serious and looming problem of climate change and to that connected with the progress of the production of energy from renewable sources.

In the 2018 edition, maximum attention was given to employment problems along two lines:

> *The formation of new green jobs*

> *Job losses in the transition.*

More in-depth is the analysis of the green evolution of the Italian economy which is articulated in the Report by sectors and which refers to an updated processing of the main indicators.

The texts ended with a note that went to expose the policy proposals developed by the National Council of the Green Economy and re-launched by the General States with a declared destination for the government and political forces that would come to Parliament to follow.

World trends

The international environmental priority for the green economy is the climate that is not following a good trajectory.

Three years ago there was an unexpected 1.5% increase in carbon emissions from the burning of fossil fuels for energy purposes at a global level, even then 2018 was not promising well ... and at the current pace it is becoming increasingly complex to implement the Agreement Paris.

Already this table knew the causes of climate change that were not evident from 2017 but from before:

- ➤ *reduced biodiversity,*

- ➤ *increase in extreme events,*

- ➤ *climate migrants*

on this last point, the 2016 figure told us that migrations due to the climate in 2016 alone accounted for 76% of the 31 million displaced people.

The focus was (then as today) on China where, although there have been ambitious programs on renewables, it is expected that they will have to reach 200GW of solar by 2020, which as we know has not been achieved and (at the same time) continues to burn coal, in fact, in 2017 carbon emissions increased by 3.5% and in the first quarter of 2018 they rose by 4% compared to the same period of the previous year.

These negative international trends follow a period of stable and promising containment of emissions, once again highlighting the need to provide climate and environmental objectives with a substantial economic and monetary "payment" with investments, technological development and innovation.

Alongside the increase in carbon emissions, there is also a constructive figure:

Without prejudice to the difficulties, the skepticism of some (many) governments and the restraining force of brown industrial interests, renewable energies were increasing overall in 2017.

"It is clear today that the relationship between businesses and the environment is changing," said Davide Crippa, Undersecretary of the Ministry of Economic Development to the General States.

"In their business models, companies are increasingly incorporating environmental issues, not surprisingly in Italy green companies represent 27% of the total, a percentage that rises to 33.8% in the manufacturing industry."

source: ren21 2018

Funding for transition to the green economy

The first great opportunities in international financing were created precisely in the field of renewable energies: the first and important investment flows, both national and international, have increased more than quadruple since 2005.

source: ren21 2018

In 2015, most of the funds went to projects related to:

➢ *wind power (38%)*

➢ *solar (56%).*

Globally, annual investments aimed at generating energy from renewable sources have outperformed investments in fossil fuels, mainly thanks to the rapid drop in technology costs.

In 2017, the global figure for new investments was $ 280 billion.

Then new opportunities arose to finance projects related to the green economy, such as the increase in the number of financial institutions that were issuing green bonds.

The United Nations Environment Program - Unep in 2014 gave rise to an international project called Inquiry through which it was possible to support national and international efforts aimed at moving the huge investments necessary to promote a green economy that it is inclusive.

Another measure was that of the "Fossil fuels divestment" initiative or an action aimed at discouraging investments in the fossil energy sector and in favor of another more efficient and effective one: that of renewable sources.

For 2017, more than 800 institutional and private entities have divested 6 thousand billion dollars from fossils.

The green economy and employment

UNEP still supported and still claims that the green economy represents:

A): a quality job generator (decent),

B): adequate wages,

C): suitable and safe working conditions,

D): stability for the workplace,

E): reasonable career prospects

F): rights for workers.

These data come from the source: Irena 2018

According to a study from the United States, renewable energy and low-carbon sectors generate more jobs per unit of energy produced than the fossil fuel sector, but what is most striking about the analysis is the great change in the efficiency of job creation in investment breakeven.

Data:

- *In 2017, solar PV marked a record year for employment which rose by + 8.7%.*

- *The wind industry employs 1.1 million people worldwide.*

- *Biofuels employment is estimated at 1.93 million with a figure of + 12%.*

It is clear that these global changes ask for and manifest themselves on sectoral and regional differences much more when the creation of new jobs in a sector such as renewables will generate a loss of employment in fossil fuels.

Estimates say that the creation of 18 million jobs scheduled for 2030 is the result of about 24 million created and about 6 million lost.

Trends on a national basis (country by country)

Italy in the green economy (before these last governments) was an excellence on the theme of the circular economy but it goes very badly for the consumption of soil as seen and said.

The 2018 Green Economy Report revealed an update regarding the performance of the strategic sectors of the green economy in Italy, recording excellence and falls.

Other data on employment in the green economy of 2017 said:

➤ employment in renewable sources with 32% of the total employed (approximately 702 thousand direct and indirect jobs),

➤ jobs in organic and quality agriculture with 18% of the total employed (about 393 thousand jobs, in this case only direct),

➤ in the urban regeneration sector with 12% (around 255 thousand jobs),

➤ in the efficiency of buildings with 9% (over 197 thousand workers),

➤ in the redevelopment of the water system with 8% (approximately 178 thousand jobs),

➤ in the remediation of contaminated sites with 5% (about 117 thousand jobs).

➤ In the waste sector as regards the transition from linear to circular economy with 5% of the employed,

➤ for and in sustainable mobility and eco-innovation (together) with 2% of jobs,

➤ in the prevention of hydrogeological risk with 0.7% of the employed.

If preliminary estimates were observed in 2017, greenhouse gas emissions in Italy continued to increase, but in the previous 4 years and taking into account a modest economic recovery, the process of national decarbonisation, and throughout the rest of Europe, had stuck.

In the three-year period 2014-2017, with a modest economic recovery, energy consumption began to grow again, going from 166 Mtep to over 170 Mtep and going to mark energy efficiency policies.

In 2017, renewable sources went to meet 17.7% of energy needs.

Following a period of average growth that occurred in the period of time: 2005-2013, to date the progress in renewables has traveled more slowly, even if the data of the first half of 2018, which was very rainy precisely due to the climate change, indicated that hydroelectric production had started growing again.

The energy savings obtained from energy efficiency interventions, and sustained by tax deductions between 2007 and 2016, have reached 430 ktep / year; investments activated in the three-year period and up to 2017 reached approximately 9.5 billion euros and the total amount of investments activated in 2016 was over 3.3 billion, 7% more than in 2015.

Among non-renewable sources, water should be mentioned because in Italy the situation of water network leaks which taken by analyzing 116 provincial capitals is still extremely critical, with an average of 38.2% of water introduced into the network which does not reach the 'users.

For circularity rate, the same country stands at 18.5%, in first place among the five main European countries and has a moderate productivity of material resources, measured in euros and on GDP per kg of resources consumed, it falls to the second placed among the five main European countries.

For 2016, 13.55 million tons of municipal waste were recycled in Italy, for a share of 45% and this allowed the country to rank second in Europe just below Germany, increasing by one position compared to 2014, with an excellent performance (67%) in particular in the packaging waste sector.

On the other hand, Italy was among the leaders in Europe in the field of special waste recycling in 2016 as about 91.8 Mt of special waste had been recycled, for a 65% share measured on the production of said special waste.

32 provinces were also measured going to view the levels of separate collection above the target of 65%, this is how they are distributed territorially:

> ➢ 25 in Northern Italy,

> ➢ 2 in the Center

> ➢ 5 in the South.

Separate collection is practiced over 87% in Treviso, while Belluno and Pordenone are around 84%, finally Tortoli and Mantua managed to reach 83%.

On the other hand, on the theme of eco-innovation, if it is based on the Eco-IS (Eco-Innovation Scoreboard) indicator, Italy reached a score of 113, positioning itself above the EU28 average of 100, competing with different countries (exceeding only the first highlighted in the list, while for the other 4 Italy follows them):

> ➢ *Austria,*

> ➢ *Sweden,*

> ➢ *Finland,*

> ➢ *Germany,*

> ➢ *Denmark.*

Organic agriculture in 2017 reached 1.8 million hectares, increasing by + 20% compared to the previous year.

Spain is the 1st EU country per square meter occupied by organic agriculture, the 2nd country is Italy.

They are located behind Italy:

> ➢ *France*

> ➢ *Germany,*

Agricultural production of certified quality also increased in 2017 and reached a value of 15 billion at the end of 2016.

Land use in 2017, however, continued its run, at a rate of 15 hectares per day:

Italy remains among the European countries with the highest percentage of land use as mentioned.

Soil consumption, even through artificial cover and waterproofing, continues to increase.

The top 55 least virtuous municipalities are located in Lombardy and Campania with a prevalence in the provinces of Naples and Milan with 55% higher percentages of soil consumed than the entire municipal area.

However, the highest values of consumed area are located in Rome with 31,697 hectares and a further growth of 36 hectares in 2017 equal to 0.11% more and in many municipalities in the provincial capital:

> ➢ *Milan (10,439 hectares, 19 more than in 2017),*

> ➢ *Turin (8,546, with 0.2 more),*

> ➢ *Naples (7,423 with 6.6% more),*

> ➢ *Venice (7,216 with 37.4% more).*

In absolute terms, 71% of the greatest land use between 2016 and 2017 occurred in the smaller municipalities with a population of less than 20 thousand inhabitants.

Italy stands as the Pese of wild concreting.

However, taking into account relevant exceptions, public green spaces in cities have a very low value of around 5%, in 96 of the 119 municipalities in the provincial capital.

Between 2011 and 2016, the scenario appears to be extremely negative overall, with a significant decrease in the areas with public green areas.

In 2015 in Italy of the 166 billion euro share of investments in housing, 119 billion equal to 73.1% related to the ordinary and extraordinary maintenance of the existing assets, while the new buildings were equal to 26% of the production.

Extraordinary maintenance has jumped from 77.4 billion euros in 2007 to 85.7 billion in 2016, and the new construction market is twice as big.

There is a conversion of the areas that were once an agricultural corollary, even in the provinces and small villages, the villages are becoming micro towns, losing their natural vocation and reserving limited areas, so people are removed from the countryside.

In several Italian cities, the scourge of building illegal rule reigns, increasing from 11.9% in 2005 to 19.4% in 2017.

Specifically in the South and in the Islands, it remains very high: in 2017, it reached a value of about 50%, so that every two legal homes has one illegal one compared to 5.5% in the North-East of the country.

And this question is sad considering that the natural heritage in Italy is among the most important in the world, while the expenditure for the protection of biodiversity and the landscape in Italy is very low and has decreased from 689 million euros in 2010 to 525 in 2017.

Italy and the European country where the largest share of vehicles with different power supplies than traditional fuels (petrol and diesel) runs on the total of vehicles: 12.7%, an increase of almost nine percentage points compared to Germany.

The Italian figure is supported by the spread of the gas fleet (LPG / methane), which with 3.16 million vehicles among:

> *car,*

> *light and heavy commercial vehicles*

it occupies a 53% share of the European gas fleet.

But the data remained at the stake regarding the new ecological vehicles: in the top ten of 2017 sales, neither in the category of hybrid vehicles, nor of plug-in hybrid vehicles nor in the electric ones, there is a car that was produced in Italy.

In 2017 there were only eight Italian capital cities where travel by public transport, on foot and by bicycle had exceeded 50%, here they are:

> *Bolzano,*

> *Bologna,*

> *Ferrara,*

> *Florence,*

> *Milan,*

> *Pisa,*

> *Turin.*

> *Venice.*

Instead in the European context, Rome is the city with the highest percentage of journeys made using private means with 65% compared to:

➢ *15.8% of Paris,*

➢ *26% of Madrid,*

➢ *30% of Berlin,*

➢ *37% of London.*

Italy is the European country that also had the highest number of premature deaths from air pollution, in 2016 the European limit value for PM10 was exceeded in 33 urban areas, and post Covid-19 this figure should give us food for thought as PM10 is one of the vehicles exploited by the virus to spread.

Already in 2016 for the most part the cities with the highest PM10 rate were located in the North, and 82% of the population was already exposed to average annual levels higher than the guide value for PM10 (20 µg / m³) which are indicated by the World Health Organization (WHO).

Policy proposals for the green economy in Italy (2017)

A structured package of green investments could and can still make a significant step forward in the transition of Italy towards the green economy by helping the economic and social recovery and generating new jobs which in five years could reach to exceed 2, 2 million jobs which would become 3.3 with the related industries.

Green measures on which to make investments fall, whether they are public or private, must include:

- ➢ *a duplication of renewable sources;*
- ➢ *redevelopment actions (almost integral) of private and public buildings,*
- ➢ *the achievement of new European waste recycling targets;*
- ➢ *the creation of an urban regeneration program;*
- ➢ *the doubling of investments in eco-innovation,*
- ➢ *measures for sustainable mobility*
- ➢ *measures for ecological and 0-impact agriculture;*
- ➢ *the requalification of the water system at all levels;*
- ➢ *the strengthening of the prevention of hydrogeological risk, leading to an improvement of the remediation of contaminated sites.*

All these measures would engage institutions and individuals with seven and eight billion of public investments per year, less than half a point of GDP, it had to be done in 2017, now three years have passed and the crisis has been helped by not taking into consideration a real change, precisely the one towards Renewable and Impact Sources 0.

But speaking of the hypothetical plan given that the oil and extractive lobbies have amply demonstrated that they do not want to do anything for the common good of people and of the whole planet in general, thinking selfishly only of their interests and privileges of power, it would take five years activating 21.4 billion of private annual investments, and going to generate a production value of 74 billion and on average 440 thousand new green jobs every year which, together with related activities, would reach 660 thousand and above.

There are seven programmatic priorities if it were decided to revive the Italian economy through a total transformation of the model that failed miserably by making climatologists define our time no longer as Holocene but rather as anthropocene.

These priorities have been placed in the general interest by the National Council of the Green Economy and which has turned into a political proposal addressed to the political forces of Parliament in 2017 and therefore to the Government.

The green route winds through various stages which include:

- ➤ *relaunching renewables*
- ➤ *prepare energy efficiency to face the climate challenge*
- ➤ *renewal of the energy system;*
- ➤ *start and develop the circular economy,*
- ➤ *enhance the results achieved*
- ➤ *effectively implement the new package of European directives;*
- ➤ *promoting ecological quality as a crucial factor for the success of Italian companies;*
- ➤ *ensure the development of sustainable, quality and multifunctional agriculture;*
- ➤ *change the direction of urban mobility;*
- ➤ *activate a national program for urban regeneration, which makes use of the support of tools and addresses provided by the green cities;*
- ➤ *to conserve and enhance natural capital.*

Reviving renewable sources and energy efficiency would mean facing the climate challenge by renewing the energy system that weighs heavily on pollution and climate.

The time available to the earth is not long.

During the Special Report SR15 presented by the Intergovernmental Panel on Climate Change - IPCC, the theme was to contain the global increase in the average world temperature within 1.5 ° C, in this case it was certified that we have only a few years are available to reduce temperatures and implement, without indulging in other delays, the Paris Climate Agreement.

As far as Italy is concerned, compliance with the commitments established by the aforementioned Agreement would provide for the disclosure of a medium and long-term national Energy and Climate Plan, which aims to reduce greenhouse gas emissions. 50% by 2030 and 80% by 2050, doubling the contribution of renewable energy sources by 2030 - reaching a share of at least 35%.

To achieve these results, the request was to set up a national fund for the energy transition that included carbon pricing measures such as the carbon tax, supplementing the latter with further interventions capable of promoting and directing innovation by supporting it with suitable investments both on the energy efficiency is to promote a reasonable growth of renewable sources.

Going towards a circular economy, learning to value the good results already achieved and effectively implementing the laws envisaged on the subject is the new horizon to which we must adhere as a society.

The results obtained in the waste production sector, once again taking only Italy, are very good, but in 2020 it is necessary to work to preserve and improve what has been achieved so far.

Italy must maintain and enhance the position reached among the leading European countries in the efficient use of resources and in the recycling of waste, to solidify a circular economy making it a lever for developing its green economy.

This will be possible not only through the transposition of the new package of European Directives on waste and the circular economy, but also by improving the recyclability of products and above all by developing the market for raw materials and recovered and recycled goods.

A commitment is also needed to strengthen the responsibility of producers, so that they pursue non-profit-making purposes and have detailed and specific methods for the different supply chains.

It is also appropriate to introduce re-use objectives but above all to reward those who make separate waste collection constantly, with appropriate tariffs proportionate to the quantity and quality of the waste brought in as well as to the efficient costs of their management.

Promotion of high ecological quality as a decisive factor for the success of businesses

A successful made in must provide for a high ecological quality of products and production processes.

To achieve this goal and compete in a worthy way both on the domestic market and on foreign markets, digitalization must be better targeted in some social realities, in Italy this will falls at the center of the Enterprise 4.0 Program, useful to boost the development of the green economy, with attention to small and medium-sized enterprises.

A green tax reform is also needed in order to accompany the market, both on the demand and on the supply side, meeting industrial processes and services with low emissions and high efficiency in the use of resources, promoting a reduction in the tax burden on labor and greater investments in eco-innovation.

And as a last (but not least) point, it is necessary to reward Italian companies that produce goods and services based on a high energy quality, going to provide for them an adequate simplification of administrative procedures so as to encourage more and more processes to enhance natural capital and environmental services.

Another point that should be applied globally is the following:

The development of sustainable, quality and multifunctional agriculture

To ensure adequate sustainability and safety standards, agriculture should be localized, promoting sustainable, organic and production related to the variety of cultivated species but also spontaneous and anchored to the cultural and landscape values of the place where they arise.

For this reason, agricultural areas, pastures and forest heritage must be preserved, highlighting the strategic role they play, a circular and multi-function role.

The policies should favor the agricultural and forestry sector as additional sources of energy and renewable materials production that can be used in the bio-economy which, if managed in a sustainable and circular way, thus contributing to the integration of income in rural areas and to curb the abandonment of mountain and internal areas.

In addition to these measures, it is necessary to support the active management of the forestry-pastoral heritage, working towards the planning and aggregate management of public and private properties, with a prompt promotion of economic and fiscal instruments that reward managers and companies committed to guaranteeing a sustainable production.

A change in urban mobility

We live a mobility that pollutes and congests, in some countries such as Italy the private and polluting-congestion medium is widespread enough to become the first among the means of transport used.

This model entails several inconveniences for citizens, generating very expensive direct and indirect costs for the economy and for health.

Italy is the European country with the highest private motorization rate, as previously mentioned, but the data are clear:

> ➢ *635 vehicles per thousand inhabitants*

comparing with other countries in the EU zone, here is what emerges:

> ➢ *France 555*

> ➢ *Germany 477*

Italy in the EU area also has the highest rate of premature deaths due to air pollution.

It is clear how important it is to speed up the development of sustainable urban mobility, and at the same time to reduce the number of private cars currently circulating and staying in cities.

To do this, it is necessary to focus on a transport offer that provides for different ways and approaches no longer based on the use of the private car, but on an accessibility to public transport that is lacking today and which has been poorly depleted over the years. constant and significant in favor of the private interest of accumulating profits for the few against the human communities.

Further alternatives are represented by sharing mobility, but also by the greater use of pedestrian areas and cycle paths.

The hope is to continue to support the adoption of stringent emission reductions for new vehicles at European level, defining intermediate targets for 2025, so as to prepare a sincere and effective reduction of greenhouse gas emissions in compliance with the Paris Agreement. .

To do this, the electrification of the sector must be intensified by focusing on electricity produced from renewable sources and the use of advanced and sustainable biofuels.

Activate a national program aimed at pursuing urban regeneration, supported with the tools and guidelines that come from green cities.

Soil consumption, a resource that must be remembered is limited, must be stopped.

The regeneration that cities in various places around the world must apply, guided by the principles and guidelines of green cities, is the main way to relaunch. There is still the need to activate financing and widespread paths (also on a cultural level) aimed at ensuring that the regeneration of the cities that must define:

> *maintenance projects and interventions,*

> *recovery documents,*

> *deep redevelopment (deep renovation) of existing assets,*

> *remediation and reuse of polluted, degraded and abandoned areas,*

> *promotion of urban greenery, even private,*

> *seismic and hydrogeological safety measures,*

through a national program for urban regeneration are put in place, this program should be able to involve all provincial capitals as a basis for expansion, and should be supported through innovative economic and fiscal instruments that also favor civil society initiatives, with involvement from part of all citizenship.

Protection and enhancement of natural capital

Italy is a country that has the most significant natural, cultural, historical and architectural capital of various countries.

These dimensions, natural and cultural, are the wealth of this country and also a peculiar component of well-being for citizens.

Both need to be better protected and enhanced in a way that provides a systemic contribution:

> *coordinated*

> *integrated*

in order to increase the attraction of the country and to support economic activities of increasing importance such as the sector (for example) of tourism.

An aspect little considered that should instead be taken as a signal of a wrong model at its origin and basis is that of the threat of hydrogeological instability.

> *Increasingly frequent floods*

> *Systemic landslides (hence now stabilized).*

They are the new nature, and this new nature reminds us that nothing has a fixed character as the economic model pursued up to now wanted to suggest and impose.

This problem or better, awareness must be addressed through planning and management of the territory more attentive and updated to the new climatic context and through the implementation of risk prevention and mitigation measures.

But in order to prepare answers that are worth implementing, a renewed political sensitivity is needed, which takes the environmental issue as a priority for the survival of any species present on earth, enhancing biodiversity rather than an increasingly marked model on the reduction of diversity.

Much attention must be paid to water, a precious and limited common good that cannot be wasted. A wider reuse must be promoted by guaranteeing adequate water quality standards deriving from purification and those subject to remediation of contaminated sites.

In addition, it would be more than appropriate to educate the dissemination of good practices that go towards a renaturalization and improvements of the hydrogeological networks, but it is also necessary to re-evaluate all the existing plans that require environmental recovery interventions.

Taxation policies in the EU zone

Europe does not legislate directly on the issue of taxation for the individual countries of the area that make up the EU but still provides addresses.

Currently there are many rules and regulations on the subject of taxation on individuals but also on businesses.

For example, there is a document entitled:

" Tax policies in the EU: 2020 survey"

very recent and dated March 2020

The theme of this document concerns both the Green conversion and the taxation envisaged for businesses and is called:

"Aggressive tax planning and transition to the green: the role of right tax policies"

According to the EU, multinational companies would continue their commitment to aggressive tax planning which aims to reduce their tax burden.

This assertion emerges in data collected by the Commission collected through the study "Tax policies in the EU: 2020 survey", published by the Commission itself.

The report also highlights the role that certain (and effective) tax policies can play in supporting the transition to a Green socio-economic model.

For example, in the past year in almost all Member States, the nominal marginal tax rates for diesel used in private road use have fallen compared to those for unleaded petrol, even if diesel has a higher carbon content and therefore has a higher negative impact on ambient air quality.

The European Commission has published this study: "Tax policies in the EU: 2020 survey". The analysis contained in the report highlights several aspects that need to be taken into account, for example that Member States' tax systems can become fairer and more efficient.

But that this transformation can be done through various incentives, the EU itself lists them:

> ➢ *tax incentives,*

> ➢ *reduced tax burdens for low-income incomes,*

> ➢ *tax policies to encourage social mobility and create effective tools to combat tax avoidance.*

From this press release / document also emerges a data that is saddening, that for which from the side of the tax reforms implemented in the Member States between the period of a year from June 2018 to June 2019 there is no transformation suitable for a Green conversion.

By contrast, on average, all categories of tax revenue in the EU are increasing, corporate income tax rates continued their downward trend in 2019.

The report examines European tax policies within the five priorities of the Taxation according to the European Commission, according to the analysis carried out by the Commission itself:

- ➢ *stimulating investment and tackling positive and negative externalities,*
- ➢ *The improvement of the functioning of the tax administration and fiscal certainty,*
- ➢ *The purpose of promoting employment,*
- ➢ *The reduction of inequalities,*
- ➢ *Spontaneous tax compliance insurance.*

The EU has perfectly understood that a single policy for all categories is not suitable, although some parties are pressing in this direction, according to the Commission, fiscal policies must take into account all national specificities and circumstances.

These five EU tax priorities are helpful in indicating to governments how to carefully design a mix of tax policies, which take into account efficiency, distributional effects, tax administration and spontaneous tax compliance.

If indirect taxes are taken into consideration, and particularly those on consumption, progressivity and therefore redistribution in the Member States would probably be reduced.

Since consumption taxes reach significant shares. Reaching a threshold that even reaches 50% of tax revenues in some States, this is how one senses a significant limitation. But which is the first among the EU's tax priorities? The priority is revenue, or an adequate stimulus towards investment. The report examines aspects such as reforms that are truly capable of addressing the problem associated with the distortion of tax payables in corporate taxation.

So we discuss both individuals and businesses (as anticipated). The reforms must go to limit or abolish the deductibility of interest costs according to the EU and an example in this sense is represented by the corporate income tax reform or by the rules on reduced capitalization.

Both these measures not only counteract the distorting effects of debt, but also lend effective support to investment activities. Instead, the EU's second tax priority is to improve the tax administrative system.

In this case, the report examines some indicators from the Member States such as the post-filing index, an indicator that measures the time needed to obtain a VAT refund or to correct an error in the tax return.

We must add the presence of a wide range of digital services aimed at taxpayers, in particular the opportunity to send online, on which the EU Member States have pressed so much, a measure that can reduce the costs related to compliance by making the at the same time the tax administration is more efficient and improving the so-called compliance.

The e-filing indicator indicates the percentage of individual tax returns that is sent online to the tax authorities.

The latest data available to the EU indicate improvements in all countries since 2009, but the level of e-filing is still quite low in some countries.

Instead the third and fourth EU fiscal priority is that of employment incentives and the reduction of social inequalities, the report examines some categories of workers, such as low-income ones, which are more sensitive to changes in the tax burden.

For this category, one of the reform hypotheses may be that of concentrating the reductions in labor taxes, which at the same time will support other political objectives, such as the reduction of income inequalities.

The last of the EU's priorities is that of increasing tax compliance, from the report it emerges that this aspect needs to be improved means going to guarantee revenue aimed at financing public policies such as:

➢ *education,*

➢ *healthcare,*

➢ *the infrastructure sector,*

➢ *defense and other services essential for the creation of a democratic society.*

As another point, the EU highlights the element of trust in the functioning of the tax system as a prerequisite for spontaneous tax compliance.

Remaining on the report wanted and produced by the EU, data emerges on how multinational companies continue their commitment to aggressive tax planning with the aim of reducing their tax burden and how tax policies act as a pick for playing an important role in support the transition to a Green economy.

The EU recalls that in 2019, in each of the Member States with the exception of two, the nominal marginal tax rates relating to diesel for private road use were lower than those for unleaded petrol, even if diesel has a higher carbon content and a greater negative impact on air quality and therefore in the environment.

Tax reforms in the EU: this is the topic of the last paragraph of this report.

The European Commission advances the hypothesis of fiscal policies that create a tax system based on efficiency, sustainability is equity.

Instead, taxes in the EU area have not been harmonized, coordinated commission action becomes more necessary to face the challenges that now, post-lockdown, become even more necessary.

In general (and in each sector) solutions that have been coordinated are able to guarantee:

- ➤ *competitiveness*

- ➤ *sustainability*

in this case of the Eurozone economy.

Sustainability should also be envisaged for the EU tax base, by tackling tax evasion in a more effective way in parallel, these two measures (jointly implemented) would help prevent dubious dealers and criminals from using funds deriving from the financial system of the EU, as we unfortunately know also by reading newspaper headlines from various countries.

This stealing is a problem, Italy is among the countries in which open fictitious companies are often discovered only in order to obtain public funding, including the EU, but as in Italy it also happens in other countries.

The main actions of the Commission on the subject of taxation in the last six years, i.e. from 2014 to 2019, have pursued the fight against tax fraud, tax evasion and aggressive tax planning.

The aim of these prosecutions was and is to improve tax transparency, promoting administrative cooperation and the revision of harmful tax regimes.

In this sense, the EU has set up key initiatives proposed by the Commission and adopted by the Council which imply as many strategic objectives:

- ➤ *2 anti-tax avoidance directives (respectively: ATAD I and II);*

- ➤ *5 directives which modify the directive on administrative cooperation (the abbreviation is: DAC);*

- ➤ *1 review of the patent box regimes of the Member States by the group "Code of conduct for business taxation".*

The report highlights many aspects as seen and discussed by the Commission itself, a further aspect is that relating to the package of measures envisaged for digital taxation.

This of digital taxation was a real proposal carried out by the European Commission in 2018, a proposal that provides rules to ensure that the activities of digital businesses are taxed fairly and conducive to growth in the European Union.

On 15 January 2019, the European Commission presented a communication on how to proceed gradually from the unanimity criterion to qualified majority voting in some areas of EU tax policy.

A change towards a Green Economy also passes from finding resources as we know, and from the commitment of companies towards a model that privileges sustainability instead of an egoistic value that has brought us and brought us all to the current energy and environmental upheavals.

Company taxes (EU proposals)

For many years in the EU area there have been discussions of proposals that lead to the harmonization of corporate taxes. Here are some reports on the topic:

> *Neumark report dated 1962,*

> *Van den Tempel report dated 1970,*

> *proposal for a directive for the alignment of rates between 45% and 55% dated 1975.*

In 1980, the European Commission ceased to accept (ideally) these proposals arguing that a harmonization procedure would never work, in this case it is necessary to go and observe the document: COM (80) 0139.

Going to put an end to this will, the EU has started to focus on measures to complete the internal market. In this text:

Guidelines for corporate taxation

dated 1990 (SEC (90) 0601) three proposals were accepted:

> *the Mergers Directive (90/434 / EEC, which is currently Directive 2009/133 / EC);*

> *the directive on parent companies and subsidiaries (90/435 / EEC, which is now directive 2011/96 / EU)*

> *the arbitration procedure convention (90/436 / EEC).*

Since 2001, the EU has been following the "state taxation of residence" project for SMEs (small and medium-sized enterprises).

This project provides that the latter have the possibility of calculating their profits also those accumulated in other Member States on the basis of the national tax rules with which they have developed confidence and relating to the State of residence.

As regards the elimination of tax obstacles to cross-border venture capital investments, a group of experts was set up and presented a report in 2010.

He reminded you of how this document tells us, which gathers not only the indications for SMEs but also other types of taxation, what the role of the European Parliament is.

Compared to tax proposals, the role of the European Parliament is limited.

In essence, the EU has only the role of a consultation procedure.

The resolutions of the European Parliament have largely supported the Commission proposals which concerned and concern corporate taxes and direct taxes on natural persons, raising the request for an extension of the scope.

Parliament tends to elaborate what are defined as:

annual tax reports.

The first report was approved in February 2012 and the topic was that of double taxation problems.

A 2015 report explicitly condemned an aggressive tax policy and instead supported a common approach to more effectively tackle tax fraud and tax avoidance by associating it with an intent to improve the framework for the proper functioning of the single market.

Parliament passed two resolutions:

> ➢ *TAXE*

> ➢ *TAXE 2*

making use of a base that hinged on the work of the temporary special commissions relating to tax rulings and other similar measures by nature or for actual purposes.

In 2016, after the Panama Papers leaked, the European Parliament set up a commission of inquiry (the PANA commission) which was tasked with examining complaints of infringement and maladministration in the application of related EU law. money laundering, tax avoidance and tax evasion.

In October 2017, the PANA commission decided to adopt its final investigation report. In the same year and in December, Parliament adopted a recommendation to the Council and the Commission after the work carried out by the committee of inquiry.

In March 2018, the European Parliament established the special commission on financial crimes, tax evasion and tax avoidance (TAX3) with a (partially expanded) mandate.

In the following year (and in the same month in which TAX3 was established) Parliament approved a report based on the work of the TAX3 commission.

This essay is taken from the words of Dražen Rakić expressed in February 2020 and the text from which they are taken is the following in the link:

https://www.europarl.europa.eu/factsheets/it/sheet/80/imposizione-diretta-imposte-sulle-persone-fisiche-e-sulle-societa

The EU obviously also expressed itself on the Green Economy, and on July 19, 2019 following the pressures deriving from civil society and environmental movements, the European Commission expressed various addresses, reported on the various sites of the ministries of the various countries belonging to the EU.

The model suggested for green economic development, which takes production activity seriously, evaluating both the benefits deriving from growth and the impact on nature and the environment caused by the transformation of raw materials must be a series of measures to transform the economy itself.

The green economy is an economic form in which public and private investments have the aim and the objective of reducing carbon emissions and pollution, and in parallel to increase energy and resource efficiency, avoiding loss (further) of biodiversity preserving the ecosystem, so reads from Treccani.

This is what stands out on the Italian government website, in relation to the green economy.

Since in the last fifty years we have witnessed an important enhancement of the environmental dimension in economic analysis, many definitions of the Green Economy concept have been disseminated.

UNEP (United Nations Environment Agency) in 2010 went to define green that economy that is capable of improving human well-being without forgetting and without overshadowing social equity, while simultaneously reducing risks environmental and ecological depletion.

The European Commission defines the green economy in the COM Communication dated 2011, Resolution 363 of 20 June 2011 which indicates this description:

"an economy that generates growth, creates jobs and eliminates poverty by investing and safeguarding the resources of natural capital on which the survival of our planet depends".

The OECD or the Organization for Economic Cooperation and Development has in turn created documents and strategies favorable to the green economy and in particular in relation to green growth by referring to the promotion of economic growth which is able to reduce pollution, greenhouse gas emissions and waste, going to protect and enhance the natural heritage in its cyclical continuation which allows us to guarantee resources and environmental services on which our well-being is based.

Always citing how the current government does, Treccani.

The energy sector occupies (of course) a considerable place in the hypotheses that can alternate on the issue of the transition to the Green Economy.

This kind of economic model must go to promote economic, legislative, technological and education-related measures, which pursue the reduction of the consumption of:

- territory

- power

- and all natural resources

reducing greenhouse gas emissions, gradually decreasing (and reaching zero) pollution and committing to eliminating all types of waste at the same time by promoting sustainable production and consumption models.

In this direction, the EU promotes the Europe 2020 strategy, the objectives of which are to implement measures of the following:

- Reduction of a 20% share of greenhouse gas emissions;

- 20% reduction in energy consumption;

- Plan and prepare a contribution of renewable sources to 20% by 2020.

In the EU area, we also started talking about what has been defined as the Green New Deal, this before the covid-19 hit the entire planet due to yet another anthropocentric invasion made by man in the wild.

Climate change and the degradation of the environment we are witnessing are proof of a model that not only does not work but that endangers every species, including the human one.

To overcome this state of affairs now stabilized towards total destruction, Europe needs a new strategy to transform the Union into a modern and functional economy in terms of resources and competitive together according to the directives that the EU itself intends to prepare. , these directives are summarized as follows:

- in 2050 net greenhouse gas emissions are no longer generated

- economic growth is dissociated from the use of resources

- no person and no place is overlooked.

The Green Deal or Green New Deal of the EU area should be taken on by all the countries of the European area, but we know that often the countries individually sign treaties and then not apply them at a judicial and cultural level in the societies they live in.

But the EU still has a roadmap to make its economy sustainable. Europe wants to commit itself to the objectives listed above by converting climatic problems and environmental challenges into a chance that allows it to be applied in every political sector and a transition that is inclusive for everyone.

The EU has compiled a list, or rather an index that sets the main points of this green strategy, here they are:

- ➢ *Actions*
- ➢ *History*
- ➢ *Political sectors*
- ➢ *Announcements*
- ➢ *Documents*
- ➢ *Related links*

The activities that the European Commission plans to implement for a conversion to the Green Economy include the detailed programming of a European Green Deal which makes use of a roadmap with actions aimed at:

promoting the efficient use of resources by moving to a clean and circular economy

restore biodiversity and reduce pollution.

The horizon that the current European Commission has set itself (and which has also raised considerable controversy) is that of 2050 for obtaining a zero climate impact.

The EU has made a proposal for a climate law by transforming political commitment into a legal obligation and an incentive for investment.

To carry out this aim, coordinated action by all economic sectors is needed, here are the measures:

- ➢ *placing money in environmentally friendly technologies*
- ➢ *support the industry starting from innovation*
- ➢ *introduce forms of private and public transport that are clean, cheap and healthy*
- ➢ *eliminate coal from the energy sector*
- ➢ *invest in greater energy efficiency in buildings*
- ➢ *collaborate with international partners in order to prepare improvements on global environmental standards.*

The European Union has also provided for appropriations to be allocated to technical assistance in order to financially support the people, businesses and regions most affected by the transition to the green economy.

He defined these donations under the name "mechanism for a just transition", useful to help mobilize a minimum of € 100 billion for the 2021-2027 period in the worst affected regions.

It is also necessary to take a look at how the EU organized itself chronologically, because this summary allows us to view the concrete actions put in place by the Commission:

> *First of all, there was the Presentation of the European Green Deal*

> *In early 2020, the EU launched the presentation of the European Green Deal investment plan and the mechanism for a just transition*

> *In March 2020: a proposal for a climate law emerges that will guarantee a European Union with zero climate impact by 2050.*

> *As a 4th step, the EU has opened a public consultation which closed recently (on 17 June 2020) and which concerns the European Climate*

Pact and which will bring together: regions, local communities, civil society. Companies and schools, this consultation was also launched in March 2020.

> *Staying on this month, the Commission has adopted what is defined as a European industrial strategy, to which it added a plan for the economy.*

At this point some time passes taking into account also the fact that the EU has opened a public commission that has had a long duration.

But the EU nevertheless continued as follows in the timeline:

> *Subsequently, the European Commission envisaged the proposal for an action plan for the circular economy which is based on the sustainable use of resources*

> *Then came the presentation of the "From producer to consumer" strategy useful for making food systems more sustainable*

> *And finally, very recently the EU has prepared a strategy inherent in the issue of biodiversity and its protection, giving itself the 2030 time horizon and suitable for the protection of natural resources most in need of protection on the planet we live in.*

In a schematic way, Europe with its institutions has in fact created a political agenda which extends over the long term and which incorporates economic, social and environmental issues by bringing them together and providing measures to combat climate change and a transition towards a more fair.

The European Green Deal

The EU intends to "exploit" but in a positive way the current climate crisis to create the world of tomorrow that no longer excludes the combination (inseparable and is now under everyone's eyes): accumulation of money for the few and a usurped and abused environment.

But what do the terms Green New Deal actually mean? And what do they provide in summary?

Before going into what is written on EU documents, I try to clarify what the Green Deal is.

I start with some questions:

- ➢ *How does the Green New Deal unfold?*
- ➢ *What do you expect?*
- ➢ *What is the meaning of the term?*

The sustainable idea of the European Union started recently, so these questions appear more than legitimate today.

To better understand the epoch-making significance of this environmental change that the EU Commission registered by Ursula von der Leyen wants to start, just look at the strategic objective of the plan which is to modify the old continent in the first block of zero climate impact countries in an arc storm ranging from 2020 to 2050.

On January 14th, the European Parliament gave a boost to the first stage of this important bill.

The plenary approved the (large) investment plan to carry out the sustainable transformation of the Member States.

To really understand what the Green New Deal is, what it foresees and what its appropriate and necessary impact is, we need to investigate the economic and financial impact that it will have for the production systems of the individual countries belonging to the European Union.

The commitment that the EU wants to employ assumes a certain importance on two aspects:

- ➢ *the production of visible effects on the economy and taxation*
- ➢ *the production of effects on the world of work.*

Green New Deal the meaning

Translated the terms mean: "new green pact".

So this definition is broad-based and expands.

On the other hand, as soon as she took office in the presidency of the European Commission, Ursula von der Leyen immediately made it clear that the environmental challenge would be a priority on the EU agenda.

The meaning of the Green New Deal is therefore (not literally but in practice) to respond through concrete measures of the emergency that climate change poses.

For the first time, a law binding all European countries in the EU area has sanctioned the achievement of neutrality of polluting emissions by 2050.

The rules are designed to promote a fair and just transition towards a sustainable economy that achieves a zero environmental impact in all member countries.

The focus will mainly be on achieving a balanced transformation that leaves no citizen or citizen and region of the EU bloc behind.

Ursula von der Leyen, knowing that this program is decidedly ambitious given that it is a change required by individual states, wanted to present the project by accompanying it with reassuring words, here they are:

"The European Green Deal is our new growth strategy. It will allow us to reduce emissions and create jobs. "

Vice-President of the European Commission Valdis Dombrovskis also discussed what the words mean: Green New Deal, going on to underline that:

"A green Europe will not see the light of day. Putting sustainability at the center of the way we invest requires a change of mindset. We are taking an important step to achieve this. "

The objectives of this project are specifically that of allowing the law to allow a decarbonisation of the energy sector, given that coal represents 75% of polluting emissions.

A New Green Deal that does not take this aspect into account can be understood that it cannot be considered a "new model".

The transformation must also concern the entire industrial production system.

Reforming the entire sector and becoming world leaders in the green economy is the most important objective of the law.

Mobility is also placed under the magnifying glass of the EU which calls for a rethinking in terms of sustainability.

Transport is responsible for 25% of the polluting emissions on the European continent.

These data tell us that it is essential to rethink the means of travel in EU countries to impact the environment as little as possible.

Finally, the project must also concern the construction sector, asking for a change towards the construction of new residential buildings and the maintenance of existing ones with a view to saving energy.

All EU countries belonging to the European state will be involved in this green revolution. The meaning of the Green New Deal, in fact, is currently to start a community journey that leads to zero emissions.

Of course, financial support will be structured based on the current economic structures of the states.

The economies that today are more dependent on coal and fossil fuels, such as the Eastern bloc - with Poland at the forefront and very opposed to the project - will receive more funding to convert to a model that gives a future at all.

The EU has obviously expressed a very in-depth document on this issue which is now becoming increasingly pregnant.

A communication that manages to illustrate a Green Deal for the European Union and for citizenship.

We understand how the EU is working to tackle the problems arising from climate and environmental change, preparing a task that defines our current generation.

With each passing year the atmosphere is warmer and the climate changes.

Specism and current Environmental Movements

The exploitation model that we are experiencing and that industrialization has initiated is a speciesist, to the point that the Holocene or the geological phase we are experiencing has been renamed by experts as Anthropocene: anthropos means man therefore identifies the sex of a single species out of 8 million existing species of which we are endangering the existence of at least 1 million of them with this model we have chosen.

And in addition to animal species, we are witnessing the effects of this model that pour into the environment, generating pollution and destruction of forests and oceans.

The European Green Deal intends to act as an answer to these challenges.

It is a new growth strategy that aims to transform the EU into a just and growing society, equipped to exercise a modern, resource efficient and competitive economy that in 2050 will no longer have to generate gas emissions greenhouse effect and where economic growth will be dissociated from the abuse of finite resources.

It also aims to protect, conserve and improve the EU's natural capital and to protect the health and well-being of citizens from those environmental risks and the consequences they generate.

At the same time, this kind of transition must have the character of equity and social justice.

The EU is called to put the environment and people first by giving particular attention to the regions, industries and workers who will face the greatest problems.

This will happen because the transition will bring about very important changes, so the active participation of citizens and trust in the transition are fundamental for the policies put in place to work and be accepted.

We need a new pact that manages to ideally and effectively bring together (a change of culture that eradicates the precepts that have so far been perceived as absolute) citizenship, not canceling but instead enhancing all the diversity and involving various social actors in this process which it is truly revolutionary:

- ➢ *national authorities,*
- ➢ *regional authorities,*
- ➢ *local authorities,*
- ➢ *civil society*
- ➢ *the industry,*

They will have to work in synergy and eliminate any form of selfishness, therefore in close collaboration with the institutions and advisory bodies of the European Union.

As a community, the EU has the capacity to transform its economy and society by directing its activities on a path that is sustainable.

The EU is not totally without tools as many detractors think since it can leverage its strengths as it is a world leader in climate and environmental measures, consumer protection and the rights of those who work.

A reduction in emissions creates a challenge that will require massive public investment and greater efforts to channel private capital towards climate and environmental interventions, while avoiding dependence on unsustainable industrial practices.

The European Union must be at the forefront of coordinating international efforts towards creating a congruent financial system that promotes sustainable solutions.

This initial investment (supported by a lot of money) also represents an opportunity to start Europe steadily on a new path of sustainable and inclusive growth.

The EU's Green New Deal will speed up and support the transition needed in all sectors.

The ambition that the Green Deal brings in itself cannot be materialized by Europe if it acts alone.

The factors based on climate change and related to the loss of biodiversity have a wide range since they are expressed on the entire planet, canceling the national borders always placed by the human species.

The EU can keep its influence and competences in place by using its financial resources to mobilize neighboring countries and partners to try to induce them to follow this sustainable path together.

However, the Commission continues to be an advanced area in interventions in this area, as mentioned, and it does so also by attempting to form alliances with those who intend to pursue the same objectives.

However, bearing in mind at the same time that there is a need to preserve security with regard to supply and competitiveness, even if others are not available to assume any civil liability.

This type of communication promoted by the EU refers to an introductory roadmap to policies and measures necessary to implement the Green Deal in the area to which it belongs, which will be updated according to the needs that may emerge and related strategic responses.

Every action and policy implemented by the EU will aim to contribute to the implementation of the European Green Deal.

The problems to be treated are certainly not problems to be taken individually and isolated from each other, rather they should be interconnected:

> *economy*

> *finance*

> *extractions*

> *reductions*

> *water and energy supply*

> *reuse of resources*

> *end of non-renewable policies*

> *adequate use of land and food resources*

These are complex problems.

The answer of politics must be the same, complexity does not mean impossibility as for many years it has been believed.

An important coordination is needed which is aimed at enhancing the possible synergies in all the sectors in which action will have to be taken. This Green Deal integrates other measures already previously desired:

> *2030 agenda*

> *the United Nations sustainable development goals*

> *further political guidelines promoted by President von der Leyen.*

Some highlights that the EU intends to cover are the following:

> *The transformation of the European economy to achieve a sustainable future*

> *The development of extremely transformative policies*

If the EU really intends to implement the Green Deal in its geographic area, it must rethink policies for the supply of clean energy and apply them to all sectors of the economy:

- *industry,*
- *production,*
- *consumption,*
- *infrastructure (small, medium and large),*
- *transport,*
- *food production,*
- *agriculture,*
- *building,*
- *taxation,*
- *social benefits.*

To be able to achieve these objectives, it is essential to increase the value that we attribute today to the protection and restoration of natural ecosystems, taking into account the sustainable use of resources and a drive to improve human health and all other species existing on the planet.

And I write this because in nature the species are not isolated from each other as the vulgar speciesist would like to believe in his racist being.

It is in this context that a radical change is necessary and potentially more beneficial for the EU economy, society and the natural environment.

In addition, the Commission should promote, and support through specific investments, the digital transformation avoiding electromagnetic pollution because this is also a kind of pollution, however, going towards essential tools that help to make the necessary changes.

If, on the one hand, all these sectors of intervention are strongly interconnected and should tend to mutually reinforce each other, on the other hand, it is necessary to pay close attention to the potential compromises between the economic, environmental and social objectives.

The Green Deal will have to employ many political levers:

- ➢ *regulation,*
- ➢ *applied regulations,*
- ➢ *investments,*
- ➢ *innovation,*
- ➢ *national reforms,*
- ➢ *dialogue between the social partners,*
- ➢ *international cooperation.*

Social rights should guide interventions in order to prevent someone from being excluded from the process that the EU intends to implement.

New measures are not enough even if they are to achieve the Green Deal objectives in the EU area.

The policies will be applied but these are declarations of intent and not real measures, at least they will not be until they are transformed into concrete actions.

Swedish activist Greta Thunberg who started the Fridays For Future movement with her protests over the law promoted by the EU spoke to the Eurocamera saying:

"We will not allow you to surrender."

According to Thunberg, the Executive text is based on an insufficient CO_2 balance that provides little chance of limiting the rise in global temperature.

Timmermans vice president of the European Commission replied to the Swedish activist:

"We have another approach, we will do it"

Thunberg's words are, as always, very direct and place a boulder on the intentions of the EU.

The activist claims that there has been a surrender by Brussels on the EU climate.

Claiming that she surrendered in the face of the Paris agreements, promises and all that can be done to ensure a better and safer future for future generations.

The Swedish environmental activist identifies a real failure across the board in the third pillar of the Green Deal presented at the Berlaymont.

Invited to Brussels, in the speech before the European Parliament's Environment Committee, the young Swede speaks of the ambition announced by the EU to become leader in the challenge of climate change. In the text, however, no mention of that ambition.

According to Thunberg:

*"When your house burns, accuse, don't wait a few years to put out the fire.
Yet this is what the European Commission is proposing today. "*

The activist focuses attention on times that are too long for her (and not only for her) taking into account that climate change is present today.

At the time when the EU presents this law with concern for the climate, and having the primary objective of reaching the zero emissions quota with 2050 as its time horizon, the activist recommends cutting carbon emissions immediately, remembering that there is no time to waste.

The meeting between the young Thunberg and the President of the European Parliament Sassoli produced various statements, the activist recalls that:

"We don't just need single targets by 2030 or 2050" but the European Union must aim for each coming year. Going to set targets and long-term goals, on the other hand, will not help, because in a short time there will be a depletion of the Co2 budget available to us before reaching the 2030 targets ".

Thunberg (who is based on scientific data to support what she claims) believes the Commission's text is based on an insufficient CO_2 balance which provides less than a 50% chance of lowering the rise in temperature. overall and remain below the average of 1.5 degrees.

The seventeen-year-old activist is also peremptory that the approach to climate change sees the need to be based on scientific data and bases, without which it will be very complex to prepare an environmental policy that meets the challenges that nature poses to us.

The truth according to Thunberg, is that Europe lacks the fundamental awareness and strong leadership to contrast the situation in which we find ourselves, and is pressing:

"We are in the midst of a crisis that is not yet perceived as such".

Nor does it spare the decision of the Commission and Parliament to continue investing in fossil fuels, especially through the so-called projects of common interest (Pic).

How can you think of being a leader in the fight against climate change, you ask, continuing to invest in projects related to fossil resources?

But in fact Thunberg analyzes what is in fact an uncomfortable truth, that is, that we need to change our behavior and our society by totally overturning the model hitherto supported also economically.

But because the activist speaks of surrender, it is clear from some described element, but there are not only the elements that I have highlighted so far, according to the young woman the longer Europe will continue to postpone, the more difficult it will be to go against the 'target.

He also speaks directly to MEPs saying to them:

"The European Union must be the leader, you have a moral obligation to do it and you also have an opportunity to become a true climate leader."

Any other alternative for you represents a surrender and reads the document just as a surrender.

The Commission obviously replies.

The college of commissioners, who invited the young Swedish activist to take part in the meeting, is not discouraged, replies:

"Do you not agree with our proposal? Okay, let's take note of it "

This response is provided by the executive vice president for the Green Deal, Frans Timmermans, continuing:

"It is more ambitious, it seems, but we all work for the same goal"

Timmermans claims that Greta Thunberg bases her considerations on the 'carbon budget', or on the index of the quantity of CO_2 that can still be emitted into the atmosphere before the threshold of 2 degrees Celsius increase in global temperature is exceeded, taking into account that it would be the point of no return for the balance of the planet.

Based on this assumption, more should be done now, because according to some scientists and non-governmental organizations it seems that only 1.240 billion tons of CO_2 remain at the point of no return.

Timmermans presses:

"We have another approach, and that's what I tried to explain to Greta"

The will of the EU is to focus significantly on advanced industrial solutions.

"We are far more optimistic than you about emerging new technologies."

In addition, initiatives in the economic field, such as the border tax, aim to discourage the rest of the world from continuing with unsustainable practices.

In fact, the approach of activist Greta Thunberg and of the movement that supports her and supports her own request, is different from that of the EU, and the words that follow from the current (2020) Vice-President of the Commission underline this:

A speciesist approach returns in these words, which effectively to environmental movements such as that born from Greta Thunberg's activism, is missing, and indeed is condemned.

Finance and Climate Change

Many newspapers and magazines talk about Climate Change and how the economy should take it into account.

There are various approaches on the subject.

A first approach tends to minimize the problem.

Another approach still denies it and attributes it to the action of individuals when pandemics are triggered, it seems absurd and yet there are those who attributed for example the covid-19 not to the spillover caused by speciesism and anthropocentrism but to Pope Francis, a position ultra conservative and sovereign, which however exists and in fact is a negationist of the human responsibilities that fall precisely in that phenomenon called anthropocentrism and speciesism.

Then there is the approach of the EU that splits living species wanting to privilege only one (ours) as if our species did not inhabit the earth which also inhabit other animal species as well as plants and minerals from which we are not divided.

There is also the semi-denialist approach, and this too minimizes the extent of the problem deriving from a social, political and environmental model that has depleted resources and would like to continue on this path.

Finally there is an approach that connects all the topics: environment, politics, society and sustainability, mutuality and so on and that would like a serious change of pace that renounces an industrialization responsible for an approach to the existing consumerist and not capable at all to look to the future if not for some who claim to continue to accumulate (money and well-being) in spite of the majority of the planet, in full.

It is understood that the economic ideas of the different approaches are in turn very diversified.

According to a national newspaper in Italy, the discussion begins by talking about the fact that the increase of two degrees centigrade in temperature would not be a serious problem as science claims.

However, for a part of Italian finance to the 2015 Paris agreement, the 2 degrees Celsius seem to be the goal within which to maintain itself and no longer a limit relating to the catastrophe.

And it is argued that having and staying on current rates of carbon dioxide production from human activity, the United Nations has predicted a temperature rise of almost 4 degrees centigrade by the end of the century.

The idea of catastrophe therefore changes.

Immigration defined as environmental is already substantial today, and caused by the erosion of the beaches or by very intense climatic events, as erosion is, on the other hand, examples are the desertification of areas that previously housed green areas and cultivable on small and medium scale.

According to financial experts it could be even worse: in the most pessimistic scenario it is suggested that we could reach an increase of 8 degrees centigrade compared to the average.

But the forecasts do not take into account further variables, such as:

> *the reduction of the reflective surface of the ice.*

the Earth from this phenomenon would obtain more and more ability to absorb the heat of the Sun, going to further increase the temperatures. The consequences are exacerbated by each additional degree that may occur:

> *end of many forest areas,*

> *reduction of the natural absorption of carbon dioxide,*

> *increase in the amount of methane in the atmosphere,*

> *dissolution of permafrost (which already alarms experts)*

On the other hand there are opinions (and answers) to criticisms and to these scenarios.

According to Banca Etica (Italy), for example, climate change and finance can be tackled in their binomial, in a different way.

This Bank, which has also made ethics its own appellation to underline the actions taken, reports the recent analysis made by the European Central Bank showing how climate change can affect financial stability.

The scenario of the analysis starts from scientific information that suggests how important it is to manage global warming effectively, in the coming decades we risk losing the balance of the seasons, the beauty of our places, the uniqueness of many animal and vegetable species which are still present on earth today.

The planet is facing an epochal challenge.

According to Banca Etica every person can do something to mitigate this risk, including the world of finance.

Etica Sgr is at the forefront on the issue of climate change and in general on the environmental issue. Promoting an environmental approach that is always evaluated also in the social and governance dimension (ESG).

Today the theme has a mainstream character.

The World Economic Forum every year creates a report listing all the major global risks facing the world from a social, political, economic and financial point of view.

What emerges from this and other reports is that in the last decade global risks in terms of the probability of the occurrence of dramatic events are increasingly environmental.

Today is also added the covid-19 or the nineteenth crown virus that affects the human species, to this scenario, it is true that epidemics have always existed but many of them have been caused by human hands that have altered the balance existing in nature (read anthropocentrism).

Francesca Colombo, Head of Analysis and Research of Etica Sgr at the 2019 Salone del Risparmio wanted to talk about the focus that has been created on the issues of climate change and how finance can take this problem and turn it into an opportunity.

The European Central Bank has published an analysis on:

> *climate change*

> *finance.*

The emerged conclusions have a characteristic, that of urgency.

According to the analysis carried out, climate risk has a serious negative impact on the financial statements of financial institutions and, therefore, can become relevant for financial stability, in particular if the markets tend not to calculate (as I often do, I add) correctly the associated risks to the theme.

According to Colombo, investments should be made in a more in-depth analysis and in improved communication with respect to these risks and their relevance for the financial system of the euro area in general.

The growth of information should be introduced in a clear framework, which serves as advice for market operators who must assess financial risks and position financial flows.

Europe is read in a positive way, Colombo claims that it has mobilized by preparing policies to support the transition directed towards an economy that reduces carbon emissions and manages the risks associated with rising temperatures.

But also Banca Etica maintains that the work to be done must be greater.

In order to obtain a correct monitoring of financial exposures to the global effects of climate change, reliable data proven and supported by scientific and comparable reports at the level of economic sectors or in relation to individual exposures are required.

Physical and transition risks related to climate change are another issue to be seriously considered.

Climate change and finance lead to physical risks as they lead to an impact that results in environmental catastrophes, which become economic and social and then geopolitical disasters, and all today are frequent and of a certain severity.

It is estimated that in the last thirty years the share of losses attributable to environmental and climatic catastrophes has always increased and with a constancy that has become normal.

The upward trend and together looking towards social well-being, give this scenario:

An increasingly pressing risk that in the future such losses may become uninsurable.

For example, properties in areas vulnerable to floods, fires or hurricanes and another of the issues related to the present and future scenario.

Any change that has been taking place for years now significantly increases the costs for families, for non-financial corporations and for governments.

In addition to these risks, there are also those related to the transition, which are revealed when the financial markets react suddenly to the adjustment process towards a low-carbon economy.

These risks lead to revaluations, even abrupt ones, by the financial markets.

As in the case of an unforeseen introduction relating to political measures or a rapid change in consumer preferences, which can also trigger sudden drops in asset prices for businesses and also for the relevant sectors.

The exposure of financial institutions to climate risk represents a defining point for many social actors including the EU.

The efforts that are being made by several parties to assess the exposure of financial institutions to transition risk have so far concerned the investments that should be made in some industrial sectors.

The limited analysis can be a useful tool for a first approximation of the exposure, but at the same time it isolates the specific differences of the individual sectors (examples are: processes, technologies related to production, attitude to pollution).

A comprehensive monitoring framework for risks related to climate change and finance should make use of as complete information as possible on carbon emissions and on the exposures of banks and other financial institutions.

In addition, the development of a scenario analysis and stress tests is required to face the risk of transition in a forward-looking manner and not only on the momentum.

The EU intends to make the climate targets for 2030 and 2050 more ambitious.

This is in his declaration of intent, and as mentioned the times have been taken into consideration by environmental movements, being harshly criticized.

The EU has already started to modernize and transform the economy and finance with the aim of climate neutrality.

Here are some highlights in this regard:

> *Between 1990 and 2018 effective reduction of 23% of greenhouse gas emissions,*

> *Economy growth of 61% likewise to this reduction.*

But this has been done keeping current policies, the reduction of greenhouse gas emissions will be limited to 60% by 2050.

Much remains to be done in the next decade, starting with climate action that is truly more ambitious.

The program before the covid-19 pandemic was to present an impact assessment plan for the summer of 2020 aimed at responsibly increasing the EU's target of reducing greenhouse gas emissions for the 2030 for a share equal to 50-55% compared to the levels that existed in 1990.

In order to be able to reduce greenhouse gas emissions, the Commission will also review all relevant climate policy instruments by June 2021, and will propose a revision if necessary.

Among the measures the EU foresees:

> *the emissions trading system, including a possible extension of the system to various other sectors,*

> *the objectives of the Member States in relation to the reduction of emissions in sectors outside the emissions trading scheme*

> *the regulation focused on land use,*

> *land use change and forestry.*

The Commission will propose an amendment to the climate law in order to update it.

All strategic reforms will help ensure effective carbon pricing for the whole economy.

This measure will encourage consumers and businesses to change their behavior by ferrying towards an increase in sustainable investments, be they public or private.

The various pricing tools will have the obligation to integrate each other and together ensure a linear strategic framework.

It is imperative to ensure that taxation is aligned with climate targets.

The Commission also proposes to revise the directive on the taxation of energy products, putting the focus on the environmental aspects and asking for the provisions of the treaties to be used which allow the European Parliament and the Council to adopt proposals in this sector through the legislative procedure. ordinary by qualified majority vote rather than unanimously.

As long as the different international partners do not share the same ambitions that the European Union is manifesting, the risk of a carbon leakage will remain firm, both because production can be transferred from the EU to other countries that have no interest in the environmental problem which is everyone's problem, both because EU products can be replaced by imported products that have a higher carbon intensity.

And this is one of the problems in a globalized economy that does not intend to change its model.

If this risk becomes the norm (as many analysts think) there will be no reduction in global emissions, and any intent of the EU and its industries to achieve the global climate objectives of the Paris Agreement would be neutralized.

So what to do?

Also in this case the European Commission has thought of something useful to prevent this mechanism from being skipped by countries that still deny or minimize the scope of Climate Change.

Should the scenario outlined above arise, the Commission has decided to propose a mechanism for adapting carbon at the borders for specific sectors, so as to try to reduce the risk of carbon leakage, thus verifying that the cost of imports more carefully take into account their carbon content.

This measure, which will be defined in order to comply with the rules of the World Trade Organization and the other international obligations that the EU itself has, would appear as an alternative to the measures aimed at countering the risk of carbon leakage envisaged by the system for EU emissions trading.

If you read the updates relating to Climate Change you will discover data that concern not only global warming defined in English with the terms: global warming and that is a scientific fact.

You will notice that the climatic changes connected to it are a reality in constant cyclical change as nature itself moves when it is in states of equilibrium, a balance that for too many years the human being has not allowed him to have.

This is supported by the entire international scientific community, 99% of scientists dealing with the issue of climate.

From the industrial revolution to today, then in a century and a little more, the planet has warmed by about 1 degree centigrade (1.9 ° F).

In Europe, the increase in temperature has exceeded this standard reaching +1.4 degrees, as reported by the European Union in the "Climate action" report.

The rise in temperature, which occurred in the 1950s, has accelerated in recent decades.

Each of the past three decades has been hotter than the previous decade.

Here are some alarming facts:

- ➢ 19 of the hottest 20 years ever recorded are concentrated in the period from 2001 to 2020.

- ➢ 2016 was the record year.

- ➢ Eight out of twelve months were the hottest ever, for those months.

- ➢ 2019 was, together with the previous ones and since 2015, the hottest five-year period since 1880, the year in which scientific measurements began.

- ➢ 2017 is the hottest year ever excluding the influence of El Niño, (the warm ocean current) with global climatic effects.

The critical threshold for avoiding the irreversible effects of climate change, recalls the IPCC, is only half a degree from today: limiting the temperature rise to 1.5 degrees - as required by the Paris Agreement - could make a difference on impacts.

But continuing to behave as we have done up to now, it would bring the critical threshold to 2030, in ten years (the source is always that of the data coming from the IPCC).

Half a degree will make the difference compared to the potentially catastrophic changes that will occur if the global average temperature exceeds that of the pre-industrial era by 2 ° C (in this case the data do not come from a single institution but from three which are: NASA ; the European Union; WMO).

On the greenhouse gas emissions front, only 4 words need to be mentioned:

we produce too much carbon dioxide (CO_2).

The entire scientific community or rather 97% of this agrees in considering the greenhouse gas (and in particular carbon dioxide) emissions produced by the human species directly linked to global warming.

Greenhouse gases are defined in this way because they trap the heat of the sun in the same way that the glass of a greenhouse internally preserves heat: gases capture heat in the atmosphere, overheating the surface of the planet.

The emissions are mainly due to the combustion of fossil energies:

- ➢ *intensive breeding,*
- ➢ *coal,*
- ➢ *deforestation,*
- ➢ *gas,*
- ➢ *Petroleum.*

All this gives the measure of the anthropocene or of the period we are experiencing and how a single species is totally destroying the balance for all.

Every year quotas over 40 billion tons of CO2 are released into the atmosphere due to human activities.

Carbon dioxide emissions in 2017 started growing again by 2 percent every year, after remaining stable in the previous three years.

CO2 is absorbed by oceans and forests, but only partially.

However, it remains in the atmosphere for many years.

If to date we stopped emitting CO2 in 100 years, about a third of that emitted today will still be present and a fifth will be present after a thousand years.

For hundreds of thousands of years, the concentration of CO2 in the atmosphere has fluctuated between values ranging from 180 to 280 parts per million (PPM).

In 2013, CO2 exceeded 400 parts per million for the first time in the history of measurements.

Since that year, the values have increased considerably, settling steadily above 400 PPM, an almost double value compared to the pre-industrial age and never reached before and in 800 thousand years.

The CO_2 value today has exceeded 415 PPM (the sources of these data are: NASA and Scripps).

It can be understood from the established and scientifically valid data that we are about to reach a point of no return that does not aim to scare but to inform about a truth that is uncomfortable for those who want to continue to maintain a destructive model.

What worries many scientists is the speed of the changes taking place.

Which is identified as a symptom of the planet's very delicate balances that have been altered.

We need to act immediately because we are running towards points of no return that can make the situation irreversible.

This affects not only the climate but also other parameters, such as biodiversity.

We are in the era of the sixth mass extinction, also caused by man.

The "business as usual" model, that is, the one for which the human species will continue to act as it has done so far, will lead to an increase in the average global temperature by 2100 of a minimum of 4 degrees.

With the risk of a catastrophe, which foresees rapid increases in the level of the oceans and their acidification, catastrophic alternations of drought and floods on the continental areas.

In a scenario that is instead more contained, with a heating of 1.5 degrees Celsius, the problems would be serious but we could still manage them.

The difference between these scenarios depends on a single, essential, variable or how humanity will behave.

(source: "World Scientists' Warning to Humanity: A Second Notice ")

Among the various problems of Climate Change, there is also that relating to the melting of ice.

The area that acts as a "sentinel" for climate change is the Arctic.

We can compare the Arctic to:

> ➢ _a fridge_

> ➢ _an air conditioner_

of the world for its ability to regulate the thermal of the global climate and particularly of the Northern Hemisphere.

In polar regions, climate change is progressing at speeds more than double if we compare it to the global average.

Heating is higher than in lower latitudes and every September the extent of the ice is increasingly reduced.

The polar ice cap is disappearing at faster rates, the volume of sea ice that appears to be present in the summer season has decreased by more than 40 percent in 35 years.

In 2012 this figure reached the lowest increase ever.

In the past July sea ice was 16.1% lower than the average for the period 1981-2010, the fifth lowest level ever recorded since the beginning of scientific measurements in 1979 (source: European Union).

It is the opinion of many scientists that summer sea ice can completely disappear by mid-century.

The data tells us that in 20 years an extension of ice equal to 17 times the surface of the Italian peninsula has been lost.

The melting of glaciers now goes on at a rate of 13.2% per decade.

And the ice reduction is both in extension and in thickness.

The increasingly low reflective surface is the cause of feedback (feedback must be translated as follows: "chain reaction, or cascade effect") which considerably speeds up heating:

We must speak of the so-called ice albedo

in essence and in simple terms, its ability to reflect back solar radiation.

As if to say that the more the ice melts, leaving darker surfaces to the sea and the ground, the more ice will continue to melt, further increasing the warming of the Arctic region: a vicious circle that is becoming unmanageable.

The lowering of the Arctic ice cap year after year and the opening of the north-west passage also open up new commercial opportunities.

For the passage of large ships and, above all, for the extraction of hydrocarbons such as gas and oil.

Exploitation of the latter which many propose today to combat.

In the Arctic there is a large reserve of oil, perhaps the last, which the world market has not yet used.

The governments of the United States, Norway and Russia (among others) have already opened up to new explorations in Arctic waters.

A resolution of the European Parliament asks the opposite that drilling is prohibited in this important area of the Planet which is one and is ending up under the pressure of lobbies who only want to accumulate for individuals in spite of the entire life of the Planet, these should be considered crimes against Nature and therefore also against Humanity.

In order not to jeopardize polar ecosystems already severely affected by global warming, the EU has moved and continues along the line taken.

But on the exploitation of the riches of the melting Arctic, a geopolitical dispute is already taking place which sees the three world powers as protagonists:

- ➢ China,
- ➢ Russia,
- ➢ United States.

Meanwhile Bolsonaro is doing the same neoliberal action in Brazil, violating a balance that was already compromised and not taking any scruples even in the life of the Native Peoples.

There is also to consider the theme of Permafrost with regard to the current Climate Change.

The melting of permafrost (I briefly explain what Permafrost is: it is that layer of eternally frozen soil, even submarine and represents one of the Arctic feedbacks set in motion by global warming and the melting of ice), is considered by science one of the most serious threats in the coming years.

Large quantities of greenhouse gases are trapped in that frozen area and soil, especially CO_2 and methane.

Methane is a greenhouse gas that has a wider heating effect than carbon dioxide.

Methane is a greenhouse gas over 20 times more powerful than carbon, albeit with a lower residence time in the atmosphere.

It is calculated that the permafrost is trapped 3 times the CO_2 present in the atmosphere.

Carbon and methane that would be released would accelerate global warming even more.

How quickly this process will take place is subject to further study and scientific studies.

The human species has therefore triggered a potentially fatal vicious circle here is the vicious circle:

- ➢ man-made CO_2 emissions are rapidly heating the planet.
- ➢ The heat melts the glaciers and melts the permafrost.
- ➢ Permafrost releases additional CO_2 and methane into the atmosphere which contribute even more to the increase in global average temperature.

If we stay on the water we cannot forget the issue of melting ice and heating the water which expands and stores heat going to cause the sea level to rise.

Yet another parameter that accelerates the process towards the zero point of the climate.

Up to a few years ago, on average, it grew by 2 mm per year, today the growth is +3.3 mm per year.

With an increase in sea level recorded by satellites of +178 mm in the last hundred years (source: NASA).

The island nations of the Pacific or the Indian coasts of Bangladesh are the areas of the Earth that is already experiencing the most evident impacts of Climate Change right now.

Thousands of people have been evacuated, (people who migrate due to climate change decided by very few but very powerful men in contempt of all humanity and the planet that hosts us) many islands and even cities such as Dhaka or Calcutta are likely to disappear from the all in the coming decades, being submerged due to the rising seas.

An increase in water level science predicts it between 28 and 98 cm by the end of the century, depending on the scenario.

Rising sea level is for scientists one of the most damaged and damaging climatic variables, for the so-called point of no return.

This is due to the fact that the heat stored by the oceans is excessive (93% of the extra energy released into the atmosphere by human activities) and the melting of the large masses of ice present in Antarctica and Greenland is excessively fast.

7% of the population across the planet lives in areas that are at risk.

Already in the present, extreme events and floods show us what could be the normality of many places at the end of the century, we experience them all over the place, and these become particularly dangerous in some areas.

Areas such as:

➢ _New Orleans,_

➢ _several territorial areas of Florida_

➢ _several areas of the east coast which also includes the New York area._

The increase in ocean temperatures associated with the release of CO_2 into the atmosphere which is reflected in an increase in CO_2 at sea is generating another huge impact defined by the name of acidification.

Acidification is a chemical modification that occurs in seawater and lowers its pH. Acidification is having destructive consequences on the health of fish fauna and coral reefs.

Scientists estimate that by the end of the century there will be a drop in pH of 0.4 units which could lead to the loss of 50% of biodiversity in the seas.

We must speak of real Extreme Events, extreme by the human species and by a model incapable of looking to the future, which should be changed starting from its own ideological root.

(The data from science are those of NASA Goddard Rapid Response / NOAA via AP)

Such radical events in climate change represent an indicator of the changes already underway.

These include increasingly frequent temperatures which are divided as follows:

➢ *extreme cold / extreme heat,*

➢ *intense phases of frost / heat waves.*

Waters from the oceans that get warmer and hotter are directly connected to more intense rainfall.

For each half degree of temperature higher, the increase in humidity in the atmosphere is 3%; this means that the sky fills up with water first and accumulates higher quantities which it will then have to discharge.

For many, 2017 marks an important passage on the issue of Climate Change, it is noted that three hurricanes of extreme intensity have occurred in the Atlantic, here they are:

➢ *Harvey,*

➢ *Irma,*

➢ *Maria.*

America is used to hurricanes, but never in history have two occurred in the same category 4 year.

Hurricane Harvey has generated over $ 100 billion in damage.

A subsequent hurricane that formed in the Atlantic, Ophelia, reached Europe by flooding and causing fires that left over 40 dead in four countries, and a hurricane for Europe is an unprecedented event.

The count of the disasters, however, does not stop at the events placed under the lens of the media, remaining on the same period the extreme climatic events were really many:

➢ *in Sierra Leone,*

➢ *in India*

➢ *in China*

In the latter country, the flooding of a tributary of the Yangtze River caused 310 victims.

If we stick to what science says, we must expect increasingly radical, habitual, unpredictable climatic events in their intensity.

The decisive and virulent weather events have increased in every hemisphere and in every place on the planet, especially in terms of time.

This occurred in the 1980s, an era that marked a watershed between the first (of industrialization) and the after (for events of nature that respond to this industrialization).

And the increasingly scorching climate is also advancing in temperate areas, once even Italy had a temperate climate today impossible to regain.

In a time span from the '70s (1970) to the new millennium (2012) 8,835 cataclysms related to climate change occurred, 40% of these occurred between 2001 and 2010.

(source from which this information was taken: Ejf).

In Italy from 2010 to 2020 (therefore in 10 years) almost 400 cities were affected by extreme climatic events, which resulted in 207 victims and over 50 thousand people forced to move (migrations).

The climate extremization is speeding up, it can be easily seen from the data emerged from the above-mentioned study conducted by Eif.

In 4 years, from 2013 to 2016, 18 Italian regions have been the protagonists of floods or landslides with the opening of 56 states of emergency and ascertained damages of 7.6 billion euros (in this case the data are provided by Legambiente and CNR).

Three years ago the effects of climate change were noticed with the severe drought that marked a record, but the destructive events of nature were not limited to this:

fires tripled compared to 2016.

These made a clean slate of 120 thousand hectares of territory, instead the flood of Livorno caused the death of 8 people.

Two years ago (2018) the climate alarm reached the front pages of national newspapers after the violent weather events that in 30 days caused 30 victims in these regions:

➢ *Veneto,*

➢ *Trentino Alto Adige,*

➢ *Sicily.*

Many think that we should only talk about the environmental problem, but the change that nature has taken in having been manipulated by the human being does not only concern "her".

Climate change affects (currently):

> *food supply,*

> *Health,*

> *finance and economics,*

> *access to resources.*

In 25 years, the water available per person has undergone a reduction of 26% on average, this translates into the fact that fewer and fewer people have access to this resource.

On the other hand, many governments are pushing to encourage births of people who will not have access to life, because without water there is no life, there is sadism in encouraging births to make them suffer and die prematurely of diseases and lack of access to water .

The world population is indeed growing.

A parameter that according to the scientists of the Union of Concerned scientists appears out of management, and which alone can overwhelm all other efforts for the realization of a future that is sustainable.

In 1992 the world population has increased by 2 billion people and the estimate says that it can reach a share of 12 billion individuals by the end of the century.

Science identifies a possible collapse of the system in the year 2050, also taking into account population growth.

In this limit year, we will be 9 billion and to feed us all we would need 70% more food, and the current model suggests intensive farms and intensive monocultures or food standards that destroy the land and deplete resources by abusing them beyond all measures, and which already basis represent unsustainable canons.

By 2050, the energy requirement would increase by 37% and the demand for more water would be 55%.

Translation is the total destruction of the planet by the hand of a few and an unsustainable culture, always if an agricultural, economic and food revolution does not start immediately.

Since there are fewer and fewer arable lands at present, soil erosion is advancing and droughts are becoming more serious and continuous.

There is to mention another problem related to the cultural and economic model that we have lived (in this case) for many millennia, the war as a trigger for the reconstructions made by those who led those wars:

wars are not the answer.

The climate according to the innumerable research carried out, seems to be triggering conflicts already in the present time and if we rely on the cultural model that we have lived for a few millennia, these wars will increase, associated with migrations of entire peoples, in particular from the African continent.

If it is based on research by the British NGO EJF, previously mentioned for its reliability, in 2016: 23.5 million people were forced to move due to extreme weather events. This number will grow in the coming years.

Over the next decade, global warming could bring 20 million refugees to Europe for climatic reasons, refugees who will leave from sub-Saharan Africa.

By 2100, this figure could rise to 2 billion worldwide.

A systemic emigration due to a model that started unsustainable and that has asserted itself in this sense.

They will be the new climate refugees.

Yet another related topic is that of renewable energy.

The use of these energies could contain global warming within manageable parameters, says the IPCC which is the intergovernmental group of scientists on climate change.

The latest IPCC report highlights hundreds of technologies currently available, which are low cost, and useful in reducing harmful emissions to the climate.

The report argues that it is up to governments to remove the barriers that limit the use of these technologies by going into new policies.

In most industrialized countries, predetermined energy production comes from fossil fuels and is supported economically with certain state subsidies, and the environmental impacts of its production do not reflect on the cost that end users incur.

To contain global warming within manageable parameters, by 2050 more than 50% of the planet's energy will have to be produced using sources that are renewable, while fossil fuels will have to be eliminated by 2100 as required by governments.

A goal that will be possible, according to science.

By 2050, 80% of the world's energy needs could be met by renewable energies.

Renewable energy sources should therefore become the only energy source by replacing fossil fuels, the main cause of climate change.

According to many, the Paris agreements are not enough, and we will soon see what this idea is based on.

The Paris Agreement, which was reached at the climate conference held in 2015 (referred to as COP21), is the most important political achievement in recent years.

It represented and is the first multifunctional and binding agreement on climate change.

There were 198 signatures of this agreement, corresponding to as many countries that have decided to commit themselves to accepting and practicing actions in order to contain global warming far below 2 degrees.

The agreement supported the maximum increase of 1.5 degrees. For this result, the States committed to curbing (voluntarily) greenhouse gas emissions by preparing new energy plans and national climate action plans by 2020.

Except that on the eve of Cop23 in Bonn, UNEP or: the United Nations environment agency raised the alarm.

The alarm is linked to various factors:

> *The largest producer of CO_2 emissions in history, the United States announced in June 2017 that it wanted to leave Paris and renegotiate the agreement.*

> *At a global level, urgent measures are needed.*

Much more needs to be done and it must be done immediately, not extending the actions to be put in place.

Small or slow changes are not enough.

At present (UNEP says), national commitments will only allow a third of the reduction in emissions required by 2030 in order to complete the expected climate targets.

As things turned out, a temperature rise of no less than 3 degrees Celsius is expected by 2100, with much more severe climatic impacts than we are (unfortunately) getting used to.

Financial Services and Industry

The economy is regulated by several segments which are defined by the name of sectors.

These sectors include many companies that provide goods and services to consumers.

Companies that fall into an industry provide a similar product or service.

> *For example, companies offering agricultural services go to form the agricultural sector.*

> *Companies that provide mobile or cellular telephone services fall within the telecommunications sector.*

This illustrative cross-section takes for example the financial services sector, one of the most important segments of the economy.

What is the financial services sector?

The financial services sector guarantees financial services to the market made up of individuals and companies.

This segment of the economy is made up of an assortment of financial companies, including:

- ➢ *banks,*
- ➢ *investment houses,*
- ➢ *credit institutions,*
- ➢ *Financial companies,*
- ➢ *real estate agents,*
- ➢ *Insurance companies.*

As noted above, the financial services sector is most likely among the most important sectors of the economy, and is advancing as the world leader in terms of earnings and stock market capitalization.

Large accumulations dominate this sector, as we know, but the area also includes an extensive range of smaller companies.

Based on data provided by the IMF or by the financial and development department of the International Monetary Fund, financial services are among those processes through which consumers or businesses acquire financial assets.

For example, a payment system provider offers a financial service when accepting and transferring funds between payers and recipients. This also includes accounts settled through credit and debit cards, checks and electronic funds transfers.

Financial services companies are going to manage cash flows.

Going into the merits of the topic, a financial advisor goes to manage the resources ensuring advice on behalf of a client.

The advisor does not directly provide investments or other products, but aids the movement of funds between savers and issuers of securities and other instruments.

This service represents a temporary activity rather than a tangible asset.

Financial assets are obviously not tasks. They are things.

A mortgage loan may seem like a service, but it is considered in the market instead as a product that lasts beyond the initial supply.

> ➤ *Actions,*
> ➤ *bonds,*
> ➤ *loans,*
> ➤ *consumer goods,*
> ➤ *real estate*
> ➤ *insurance products and policies*

they are classic examples of financial assets.

How important is the financial services sector in the national and global market?

The financial services sector is the main engine of a country's economy.

It provides to increase the free flow of capital and liquidity on the market.

When the sector is healthy, the economy grows and companies in this sector are better able to manage risk.

The size of the financial services sector is important for the prosperity of a country's population.

When the sector and the economy are robust, consumers generally earn more.

This macro economic circumstance increases their trust and purchasing power from a consumer perspective.

When they need to access credit to make purchases of a certain importance, they turn to the financial services sector to borrow money.

If the financial services sector loses, it can drag a country's economy down.

This condition can also lead to a recession.

When the financial system starts to go bad, the economy starts to suffer.

Capital begins to dry up as lenders tighten the bridle of loans.

Unemployment in this scenario tends to rise and wages can often go down, leading consumers to stop consuming.

In order to compensate, central banks lower interest rates to attempt to stimulate economic growth.

This is what happened during the financial crisis that led to the Great Recession.

The services provided by banks or the banking sector is the foundation of the financial services group.
This sector deals with:

- *savings,*
- *direct loans,*

instead the financial services sector brings together:

- *investments,*
- *insurance,*
- *redistribution of risk,*
- *additional financial assets.*

Banking services are provided by:

- ➢ *commercial banks,*
- ➢ *Community banks,*
- ➢ *Credit unions,*
- ➢ *additional entities.*

Banks get their earnings essentially on the difference between the interest rates charged for credit accounts and those paid to depositors.

Financial services such as these earn commission income and other methods such as the interest rate spread between loans and deposits.

Another area is that of bank splits, in which banking activities consist of several segments:

- ➢ *retail banking,*
- ➢ *business,*
- ➢ *investments.*

Also known as consumer or personal banking, retail banking is needed by consumers rather than companies.

These banks provide financial services tailored to people, including current and savings accounts, mortgages, loans and credit cards, but also some investment services.

Corporate, commercial or business banking, on the other hand, tends to deal with small and large companies.

Likewise, retail banking provides account services and credit products tailored to the specific needs of SMEs.

An investment bank usually works only with negotiation managers and high-net-worth (HNWI) individuals, not the public.

These banks sign agreements, ensure access to capital markets, offer wealth management and tax advice, advise companies on mergers and acquisitions and facilitate the purchase and sale of shares and bonds.

It should be added that financial advisors and brokers also occupy this niche.

Another and yet another sector is that relating to investment services.

People can access financial markets through stocks and bonds and by taking advantage of investment services.

> ➤ Brokers - through human or self-directed online services - facilitate the buying and selling of securities by taking a commission on their work.

> ➤ Financial advisors can charge a commission based on assets under management (AUM) but they can also direct different operations in order to build and manage a diversified and therefore more competitive portfolio on the market.

> ➤ Robo-advisors represent the latest embodiment of financial advice and portfolio management, and allow fully automated algorithmic portfolio allocations as well as commercial executions.

Hedge funds, mutual funds and investment partnerships allow you to invest money in the financial markets and collect management fees in the process.

Such organizations require custody services for trading but also assistance with their portfolios, making use of legal, compliance and marketing advice.

There are also software vendors in the market who turn to the investment fund community by developing software applications for portfolio management, customer reporting and other back-office services.

Private equity funds and venture capital providers provide investment capital to companies in exchange for shareholdings or profit sharing.

Venture capital is particularly important for companies with a technological profile from the 90s onwards. Much of what goes on behind the scenes in doing big business is attributed to this group.

Another area is that of insurance services, that of insurance is an important sub-sector within the financial services sector.

On the international market, insurance services are available for protection from death or accident:

> ➤ life insurance,

> ➤ disability insurance,

> ➤ health insurance

> ➤ against loss of property or damage

> ➤ against liability or legal action.

In the United States, an insurance agent does not take on the role of broker for example.

The first is a representative of the insurance company, instead the second takes the place of the insured and goes in search of insurance policies.

This is also the place of the underwriter, who assesses the risk of insuring customers and also advises investment bankers on loan risk.

Reinsurers are committed to selling insurance to the insurers themselves to protect them from losses that can be very large.

You will then find another relevant sector, that of tax and accounting services.

The sector brings together:

> *accountants;*

> *tax filing services;*

> *currency exchange and bank transfer services;*

> *services and networks relating to credit card machines;*

> *debt resolution services;*

> *global payment providers such as Visa and Mastercard;*

> *exchanges that facilitate operations on shares, derivatives and raw materials.*

Accountants ensure that all financial records and returns such as:

> *balance sheet,*

> *bill,*

> *financial statement,*

> *tax declaration*

are in line with federal laws and regulations and generally accepted accounting principles (GAAP).

Accountants additionally fill in the information needed to prepare entries in company accounts such as general ledger and documenting corporate financial transactions over time.

This information is used to prepare weekly, monthly, quarterly or annual closing statements and cost accounting reports.

Accountants among their duties must also resolve any discrepancies or irregularities found in records, statements or documented transactions.

In general, they observe the accounting control procedures established through an accounting system or software.

Accountants are often assigned additional finance-related tasks in addition to analyzing records and financial statements.

Instead the so-called ancillary tasks include:

monitoring the efficiency of accounting control procedures or software programs to ensure they are up to date with federal and state regulations.

Accountants also have the task of theorising recommendations to the various departments or C-suite staff regarding the efficient use of company resources and procedures.

These recommendations aim to provide solutions to financial problems or concerns that can also become very expensive.

In some cases, accountants may also prepare and review invoices made for customers and suppliers in order to guarantee assistance in timely payment of outstanding balances.

➢ *Reconciliation of pay slips,*

➢ *verification of contracts and orders,*

➢ *the construction of a corporate balance sheet*

➢ *the development of financial models or projections*

they may also be part of the regular duties of an accountant.

In addition to these tasks, accountants prepare accounts and file taxes for companies and individuals.

They analyze all the company's activities, the revenues earned and paid, or the expenses and liabilities expected to reach a total tax obligation for the year.

With the preparation and filing of both individual and corporate taxes, the accountants go ahead with a detailed analysis of tax efficiency or inefficiencies and together make recommendations on how to effectively reduce total tax liabilities in the future.

One of the analyzes of what to expect in the commercial, banking and capital real estate sectors, but also in the insurance and investment management sector in 2020 and their implications for the next decade I want to show you below by staying on the sectors examined and taking into account the pandemic that affected the entire planet.

The financial services industry is struggling to emerge from the blockade that followed the lockdown.

The report is that of 6 out of 10 employers who claim that their plans for returning to work are hampered by great uncertainty, and there is a lack of clarity on the right timing and persistent questions about how to provide an environment. safe to their employees.

In addition, half said that their employees are reluctant to return to work.

Coronavirus has infected many Americans (to reach millions on a global level), forcing many companies to operate in a remote work environment for months.

And with the new cases of coronaviruses constantly emerging, employers must completely change their plans not only based on the needs of their offices but also in order to protect the health and needs of their employees.

Among the sectors mentioned there is also the issue of the impact that COVID-19 has on banks and securities.

The global pandemic represents for many a crucial moment for financial institutions.

The crisis caused by the pandemic is first and foremost a human and environmental tragedy.

The economic impact of the crisis is far-reaching, profound and presents challenges for the financial services industry and its institutions at levels reminiscent of the worst crises of the past 100 years.

It is in this context that politics will have to make difficult choices while still weighing on the growing financial implications of the economic fallout with the serious human impact of the pandemic on customers, workforce and infrastructure.

All this must also take into account the environmental impact, and how culture (the same that leads a people to treat wild animals in almost zero hygiene and food use) affects the sustainable change that also sectors such as finance must fulfill.

The new millennium has entered silently, a crisis has been avoided, others not as we know.

Citing the steps that had been taken, the market optimism for the merger between AOL and Time Warner should be highlighted, with NASDAQ reaching an all-time high in 2000.

But that was before the dot-com bubble burst.

The following years delivered record failures, here are some examples:

> *Enron*

> *WorldCom*

with attached condemnations of some executives.

The Enron scandal has also brought down the accounting giant Arthur Andersen.

The Dow Jones closed at record time on October 9, 2007, but was soon followed by the bursting of the housing bubble, the Lehman Brothers crisis and the Bernie Madoff scandal, among several others.

In 2009, the Dow Jones marked the low of the recession going to close at 6,547, with a threshold above 50% from its maximum.

While the market has recovered and has also reached new historical highs, the injuries caused by the great recession and the constant scandals of Wall Street have left consumers less and less certain.

Consumer confidence and sentiment have gone through slight and slow growth but according to the market they remain very low.

The crisis has undermined people's trust, scandals have done the same and then there is the reality, that of the ever-widening gap between the very few rich and an increasingly large slice of the poor.

In the financial services sector, expectations but also consumer confidence fell, in America going to peak and then, as mentioned, recovering but only slightly.

After these scandals people (consumers) began to apply what we can define as "self-service" with respect to the products to choose, this choice was partly due to the lack of trust in the financial services sector.

There was research in 2012 that showed that there were 8.6 million millionaires versus 9.2 million in 2007, so the market size for many financial services companies has not grown in these six years.

Instead, the stock market reached new highs and the bond market reached relatively good targets, but consumers did not feel rich or happy because their homes and small businesses still had a lower value than the peak.

The numerous scandals that have covered all segments of the financial services sector have contributed to consumer skepticism and, on a personal level, most consumers have not achieved their financial goals.

What scenario for the future?

It is difficult to evaluate demographic changes and their impact on the financial services sector. However, it is important to examine two very different scenarios on how the industry can choose to tackle or avoid these trends.

Population growth rates have slowed, the United States is changing on several fronts:

> ➢ *age,*

> ➢ *diversity,*

> ➢ *gender.*

Population trends reinforce women's higher life expectancy.

We need to understand what the future trends in the financial services sector will be.

Some data collected illustrate many key trends with important implications for the financial services industry applied to demographics.

But what are consumers' expectations with respect to industry standards?

In terms of relationships with financial advisors, consumers are starting to expect a standard based on trust, even if they are not familiar with the terms used.

Over 75% of investors expect financial professionals I have to guarantee commission-based advice to act in the total interest of their clients in all aspects of the financial relationship.

The same percentage indicated that they would not have sought services from a broker if they had known that the broker was not required to act in the best interest in all aspects of the financial relationship.

There is also the theme relating to general trends on wealth, a theme closely related to financial services.

The gap between distributed wealth will become less pronounced with the emergence and growth of a new middle class of consumers according to many analysts.

Household wealth will change slightly as a larger percentage of consumers participate in the capital markets and when new forms of ownership emerge, such as a larger number of small businesses and shares of small capitalization businesses.

We expect institutions like:

➢ *stock exchanges,*

➢ *banks (as underwriters)*

they will gain less relevance in the years to come in terms of overall financial markets.

There will also be substantial regulatory flexibility in raising capital, which will be achieved with fewer intermediaries or levels.

This in turn will lead to more direct holdings (now called private equity for investors with substantial equity).

Intergenerational transfer of wealth.

As the baby boomers age, wealth will transfer to generations X and Y.

The largest baby boomers turned 65 in 2011 and the youngest will reach 65 by 2029.

The way financial advisors work with different generations will become fundamental.

Rothstein Kass in 2009 found that 86% of heirs in global family offices intended to fire their parent's investment advisers once they inherited their wealth.

Four new accounts are therefore needed to compensate for each lost account.

The average financial advisor is generally 50 years old, but most have no succession plans in place in the States.

In addition, only a small percentage of financial advisors are under the age of 30.

The number of financial advisors has declined in recent years and it is crucial to make this sector a convincing career choice for it being younger.

It is equally important for the greatest consultants to be able to put in place the different dynamics of the next generation of consultants, who have an orientation towards planning with respect to the product and the orientation of sales through which many current consultants have started.

Do women become the main market?

I was mentioning it just above.

Contrary to some articles in the sector, women do not represent a niche market.

Women today control the majority of personal wealth (51.3 & the data are from the United States and refer to this state).

In addition, it is expected that women will inherit approximately 70% of a large sum estimated in intergenerational wealth transfers by around 2050 (the figure in this case comes from Havens and Schervish 2003).

Women tend to live six to eight years longer than men and will need prolonged financial advice.

However, about 70% of widows change financial adviser within a year of the relative's death according to the data collected.

Female consultants represent a minimal and still too low slice, estimated at around 30% of the sector.

Another factor of analysis is that of diversity and cultural changes taking place.

Demographics show that the U.S. population is becoming more and more racially diverse, with the Hispanic population estimated to be 23% of the total by 2030 and 30% by 2050.

The younger generations are increasingly diverse.

As of 2008, 58% of millennials considered themselves white or Caucasian and 42% belonged to other ethnic backgrounds.

Social diversity is also on the rise, with an increasing number of single heads of families and gay and lesbian couples who are eligible for financial advice.

Same-sex couples need specialized financial planning to ensure that they receive the same legal benefits that heterosexual couples automatically receive.

Are there any trends that add to this data?

Indeed there are further trends that will impact the industry in the future:

- ➢ *technology*

The Internet will continue to fuel the technological revolution and online investor options will continue to grow in authority.

More than half of consumers who have a fair personal wealth believe that engagement with the Internet and digital technology has contributed to their ability to create wealth and more than three quarters believe that these will contribute to their success over five years.

Almost two thirds of wealthy investors think that collaborating with others online will be important if they want to continue accumulating wealth.

Ensuring innovative technological solutions will increasingly become a necessity and an increasing expense in all segments of the financial services sector in the years to come, and in order to optimize efficiencies and retain customers.

The technology will continue to allow more consumers to design their product offerings, while also reducing reliance on banks or large institutions.

This very direct approach allows investors to select the characteristics of an annual annuity or the secondary advisors in a separate personalized account making these practices the norm in product design.

- ➢ *Products in the future*

Product development will be influenced by the attention of consumers to the increase in tax retention and the reduction of leverage and in relation to the growth of the retirement population.

Despite a prolonged environment with a low interest rate and also with increasing rates, consumer behavior will obviously change for the future generation in terms of how savers think of low risk investments or on the basis of liquidity equivalence.

This change will include the following:

- ➢ *Need for a guaranteed return and products that generate income*
- ➢ *Continuous and accelerated innovation of paid accounts*
- ➢ *Acceleration of the movement of products towards lower total cost investment vehicles, which in the end will influence the total cost of ownership, also for actively managed accounts*
- ➢ *Growth in indexation and exchange-traded funds*
- ➢ *Continuing growth in the popularity of unbundled products (separation of recommendations from the product)*

Further trends are added to the discussion:

➢ *Request for transparency on commissions and expenses*

➢ *Complete implementation of Dodd-Frank and / or other financial services reforms*

➢ *Establishment in some form of the common trust standard for retail advice*

➢ *Higher percentage of participants in self-managed and constantly expanding pension plans; with a probability of mandatory participation in the United States by 2030*

➢ *International markets and consumers will have a growing impact on the United States and world economies*

Going even more in detail, but remaining on the hypotheses, by 2030 various scenarios may occur, I illustrate the first of many to follow.

Continuous growth in the asset management sector is driven by:

➢ *independent consultants,*

➢ *online tools,*

➢ *consulting company,*

➢ *emerging international markets.*

The financial services sector is going to consolidate thanks to mergers and acquisitions to allow economies of scale and allow success although there may be a reduction in margins.

Venture capital opportunities are varied.

Attention must be intensified on pension income, moving towards accelerated growth in investable assets due to the retirement of the pension account.

The independent channel is continuously growing and paid consultants are taking up more and more space and therefore more and more the market.

Although, the role of financial advice has evolved to make the exchange of values more transparent.

The industry in 2030 will hopefully have gone through an evolution, realizing what can be commercialized and what cannot.

Going to recognize that money is a means of achieving an end, and not a source of accumulation regardless of anything else.

In this future-oriented framework, financial advisors will need to ensure a wider range of services that require better performing customizations, including help in life planning decisions.

Trusted advisors will basically become administrators of customer goals and wealth.

Transparency will become even more essential as regards commissions and other charges, and / or explanations of the risk / reward compromises.

A fiduciary standard is the norm and consumers are most active participants in the planning and investment process.

Financial advisors and the do-it-yourself assisted channel will need to achieve collaborative leverage, which will go to the full advantage of the client.

The most successful consultants must have a truly weighted succession plan, implemented over several years to allow for a smooth transition with their intergenerational clients.

Their successors will be well educated and through the association with other professionals they will be able to provide skills in the following areas:

- *investments,*
- *insurance,*
- *tax planning,*
- *retirement strategies,*
- *wealth planning.*

They will most likely be part of a team where members develop areas of specialization, allowing the company to demonstrate effectiveness in terms of the overall planning process.

One of the many financial planning certificates, degree courses, masters or doctorates that will have to be guaranteed throughout the country and will therefore be perceived as professionals, many with specific specializations.

They will be technologically experienced and will perfectly know how to interact with potential customers and customers in different ways through:

- *Social media,*
- *direct mobile communications,*
- *collaboration in person.*

The business models and the value proposals they will propose; they will reflect the communication and technology preferences of their customers and potential customers.

More and more women and representatives of different ethnic backgrounds are entering this profession, thanks to corporate programs designed to:

> *guarantee a path provided by figures such as tutors,*
> *constant interactions with senior leadership,*
> *highly specialized training,*
> *networking opportunities.*

Tomorrow's consultants will have to lead the way by using financial education for clients and with interactive financial literacy educational games for future generations.

The communication and relational skills of women and the ability to meet company and personal needs will have to adapt to the evolving life planning model.

In addition, women are better at bridging the confidence gap; very few female consultants have been involved in the numerous financial scandals of the past few decades.

> *Insurance companies,*
> *asset management companies,*
> *investment company*

they will respond promptly to demographic changes and the digital revolution.

Going to reorganize the products to reflect more on topics such as:

> Retirement,
> Longer life spans,
> Progress in medicine,
> changes in medical coverage,
> growing long-term care needs.

They will also have to reorganize the distribution channels to make the best use of technology and interact with the growing demographic of 35-year-olds.

Self-service options are expected to become increasingly popular between this decade: 2020-2030, but as in other areas of financial services, a combination of technology and face-to-face options ensures a better customer experience.

Companies will work to understand which markets to guarantee and expand and how to provide products and services that meet their needs, balancing costs and implementations.

And here scenario N ° 1 ends, as anticipated there is not only one possible scenario for 2030, the second scenario that could present itself according to experts from the various sectors is less positive, I will illustrate it below.

In this second scenario, industry continues to be perceived by the population as negative by virtue of the continuing uncertainty of the financial services sector and taking into account the confidence gap that continues to widen.

For these reasons, investors are increasingly switching to a self-service model, excluding some consultants and even financial institutions.

In the absence of professional input and encouragement, a lower number of investors intervene to develop and implement long-term plans; others will follow up on bad decisions.

Both situations jeopardize long-term financial security.

Consultants persevere on succession planning as long as there is little time left when they make decisions that are not in the best long-term interest of their clients.

Clients who realize that a consultant does not have a succession plan will start moving by changing consultancy.

Those consultants who do not take into account intergenerational and gender differences will suffer extensive outflows of customers and capital with the intergenerational transfer of wealth.

The industry will continue to maintain and reinforce a suicidal status quo mentality and will therefore not tend to develop programs to support the next generation of consultants and clients, including women and ethnicities other than the Caucasian one.

The consultants, not going to face the growing ethnic and cultural diversity, will fix themselves on poorly served markets and push investors again towards the self-service model.

Given these two scenarios, and I stop at two, the third would be even more catastrophic than the second, and even more taxing, while a fourth would bring the issue of climate change back to the center, adapting industry and finance to life needs.

Having observed these two options, however, there is a summary and a conclusion to be made.

With both scenarios observed, the prolonged and slow economic recovery combined with the previous stumbling blocks of financial services will translate into a generation of more risk-averse consumers.

Regulatory initiatives will continue, but they are unlikely to succeed in legislation aimed at breaking institutions "too large to fail".

Demographic trends demand constant attention to pension income, elements such as:

- ➤ *Accelerated growth in investable assets,*

- ➤ *existing insurance and expansion relating to widely defined asset management services.*

- ➤ *The growth of services is likely to be driven by independent consultants, online tools and international consulting firms and emerging markets.*

Paid financial advisors will increasingly be at the center of the market, and retail banks will continue to lose power.

Resources towards the acquisition and organic growth of registered investment advisors will see a spike.

Direct distribution models are also likely to grow as consumers continue to embrace technology to help meet the needs of their financial services.

Investment management companies will look more towards international markets.

China, India and other Asian areas could become good markets for various activities in the coming decades.

The emergence of a new class of consumers in China will change the balance of economic power.

Many analysts may suggest that demography alone can generate a decades-long boom for financial services companies.

At a certain level, demographic change certainly benefits the sector; to what extent this happens, however, depends specifically on the decisions made by current leaders and on what will be made by leaders of the future.

If these strategic decisions focus on innovation and the consumer, analysts believe that the future can become the best of times.

If these decisions are concentrated more within the status quo and what is perceived as better for the sector, the future is believed to be very uncertain.

For this analysis, I drew inspiration from the words of Matt Lynch principal of Tiburon Strategic Advisors, a place from which he led numerous corporate strategy assignments for a wide range of financial services companies.

What will be the next step for the financial industry?

Some time ago there was a study conducted by NTT Data1, and from that study it emerged that 61% of financial services companies around the world believe that it is possible to overlook building engaging experiences for their clients.

A bad data don't you think?

It also represents a significant problem.

Technological developments are changing the financial services industry and, the consumer experience, defined as the customer journey, and this represents the engine and catalyst for change.

But how do you effectively engage customers?

Going to improve the customer relationship management (CRM) strategy.

Basically working on the various points of contact of the brand with which the customer interacts, and, on the places that will be material or digital, where such interactions can occur.

Advertising messages that have a centric product nature, too invasive and not very concentrated on the consumer must also be eliminated.

In such messages the dominant position is occupied by the product or service that a company wants to sell.

Advertising will have to go to another way of existing, shifting attention towards the customer.

Marketing must therefore become customer-centric.

The customer will have to occupy a central position taking care of his needs and requirements.

In this sense, it is necessary to guarantee consumers a customer experience that has a very high level, since consumer satisfaction will be reflected in the perception that the customer has of the same bank.

But it is not enough to call the customer by name or have a CRM software and a data analyst, currently much more is needed.

It is necessary to understand what are the errors in the construction of the customer journey that are currently emerging in the financial world.

In the present, the client's journey into the financial world is marked by various problems:

> * complex and unclear routes;

> * repetitive and excessively redundant steps;

> * a poor ability to monitor and track their requests and needs.

In addition, it is also necessary to consider a poor and antiquated ability to analyze data; individual Key Performance Indicators that are not in line with the expectations and needs of the end customer and also a better quality of service in the individual contact points is generally lost due to delays in transfers between departments.

It's time to meet your customers desires

If financial competitors intend to retain and attract new customers, they must find a way to keep up with their growing expectations, guaranteeing a sales experience similar or superior to tech rivals.

It is very important to understand that people do not only want a mortgage, a savings account or an investment portfolio.

People want to be able to have a home, want to see their savings pay off, and share the bill with their friends easily after dining or dining out.

People need to satisfy a need.

Which communication strategies are the most effective to put into practice?

A study, published by Springer3, noted that:

"Companies operating in the financial sector must place more resources in relationship marketing to maximize profits in terms of customer correspondence and the provision of effective services".

In simple terms, a new marketing strategy must be implemented, the relational one, which implies an assortment of tools useful to foster a deeper and longer-term relationship with current and future customers.

Personalized interactions that go towards building stronger bonds.

In short, a real CRM strategy that aims to retain customers, reduce costs and significantly increase revenues.

A strategy based on various elements must be prepared:

➢ *Knowledge of your customers*

It may seem quite obvious, but it is not at all.

Being able to really know your customers is easier said than done: in order to effectively involve people, in fact, each company must have professionals capable of reading and interpreting the data they access through the trust relationship (these data are in abundance).

It is understood that having a CRM software or an excel sheet is not enough. To date, much more is needed, if technologies have approached they have not done so on the level of trust, indeed on this level they are often proving counterproductive.

AI algorithms are also needed to analyze and process data, recognize its characteristics and can learn from their examination, receiving value.

Artificial Intelligence (AI) and Machine Learning in this way can be combined to provide financial organizations with new levels of knowledge characterized by greater contextuality, precision and speed compared to the past.

➢ *You will need to identify what really matters to the customer and the company*

The ability to personalize communication is essential if you want to create an efficient and fruitful marketing strategy.

Consumers have the desire to obtain individual experiences compared to an experience that is shared by others, therefore, consumers are attracted to highly personalized experiences because these make them feel important and unique.

In addition, personalization provides the impression that people have an individual value for the banks and credit unions that look after them.

The customer must therefore be at the center of attention and with him his needs and his needs, in fact, what is more relevant than something that touches us directly and responds to our needs ?.

➢ Product quality,

➢ services,

➢ price.

How can companies determine which of these factors are most critical to the customer segments they follow?

What are the factors that generate the greatest economic value?

Personalize and still personalize, every communication worker should repeat these words like a mantra.

Analytical tools and abundant data sources can help organizations analyze the factors that drive what customers reveal satisfies them, their behavior and, consequently, which of these behaviors creates economic value.

> ➤ *In step three you will need to apply behavioral psychology to human interactions*

<u>What can push a person to follow a certain path online?</u>

<u>Why was a user influenced by a particular communication message and not by another or by others?</u>

Asking these questions falls within the macro area defined as behavioral psychology, in essence it is being able to understand how and which particular external stimuli trigger certain answers, that is, behaviors.

Behavioral psychology is among the main tools that today's marketers use to divide the experience of their customers, identifying how external factors combine with the different traits of each person's personality, mentality, expectations and preferences, in so you can influence the decision to buy (or not) the proposed products.

<u>"Once organizations understand how their customers will behave in a specific situation, they can develop personalized experiences that will cheer customers and drive sales effectively."</u>

(quoting: Margalit, Clicktale).

> ➤ *In point 4: "Content is the king"*

Although today there are various and multiple technological innovations, a previous rule still remains valid: "if you don't communicate, you don't exist".

The problem as we have seen is that of being able to communicate effectively in today's digital world.

What is needed?

First of all, clear, direct and understandable contents, but not only, the contents must speak directly to the intrinsic need of each person, be specific and engaging based on the predictive analysis of the data held by companies.

The key if you want to satisfy customer requests is not only the measurement of what happens, but also using the data in question to guide the communication action of the whole organization, especially in creating advertising messages to be presented .

Today's consumers compare their banking experiences with those of rival banks, but also compared to other services offered by the world's most disruptive companies, including consumer technology giants such as Google and global online retailers such as Amazon who are leaders in the segmentation of consumers and in the analysis of their data.

How can you compete with the tech greats?

Going to employ their own strategy, and why not, perhaps aiming at creating a new communication path that adapts more effectively within the financial world specifically.

> ## ➤ Learn from competitors (step 5)

Learning from the greats of technology is not easy, but I want to give you an example; let's say it's 19.30, and you're coming home from work.

Go to scroll the home of your favorite site / social network and notice an interesting banner that attracts your attention because it focuses on a product and an activity you love, but this is a coincidence, you were not on your blog-site-profile social networks to search for that product, it happens because Google and others analyze you.

You will then go to click on the banner that will redirect you to the manufacturer's website.

Only that you decide not to make your purchase when you have accessed the manufacturer's site, so you will leave the site.

A few minutes later you will receive an email from the manufacturer which contains the following information:

"Thanks for visiting, we are dedicating you a 5% discount coupon on your next purchase"

you choose to open the email but do not click on it.

At this point you will open Facebook, and there you will find the sponsor of the same brand, you will find it again but this time it will suggest another product that you can easily combine with the previous one.

At this point you will find yourself confused but this confusion suits you.

Do you think the brand has excellent powers? Do you think so?

But this brand does not have exceptional profiles, it is a marketing genius, it does not even have more bank data to manage its business process that exploits the power of data for sales purposes.

Indeed it has much less, it knows very little about users.

The brand (in general I speak) does not have a more committed brand social positioning than many banks and insurance companies that go to solve people's problems and needs, have foundations, and actually invest in high social impact SMEs.

The brand simply takes advantage of what it has at its disposal, and does it in the best possible way.

➤ *The power of storytelling*

Staying on the brand, we need to talk about storytelling.

This brand has succeeded in a few moves has greatly attracted your attention, it is a fact, it has succeeded with an adequate storytelling, managing to identify your passion or a phenomenon that has an impact on the living body of society, precisely by exploiting the little information he had at his disposal.

Having this baggage he subsequently delivered this to the programmatic platforms that profiled users not only for their navigation, but also for their habits by converting such info to the right messages to a targeted audience.

Since the visit to the site, the automation of the CRM strategy has come into play, and here I am.

The CRM knows that you have visited things and automatically generates a personalized email and a coupon associated with you, in addition, it also automates the retargeting process and offers you a personalized message also on other platforms, associating potential new products with other initial products that may interest.

The e-commerce of the fashion sector, those of the sector dedicated to electronics, relating to the automotive sector, are some of the most virtuous industries that have now developed an effective CRM strategy.

Instead the financial world?

There are many proposals in the field, every single company (PMI) is looking for personal solutions, unfortunately this is a problem because it creates competitive pockets that are not always valid.

Following I am going to illustrate one of the many solutions that I want to consider.

For those who have been dealing with data and their analysis for years in the financial sector, the ideas become many, from my experience I can tell you that the solutions (as anticipated) are varied and numerous, and are aimed at solving problems who face financial and insurance intermediaries.

Themes like:

- ➤ *content*
- ➤ *CRM strategy for the financial sector*
- ➤ *management*
- ➤ *creation of branded content strategies*

aimed at the design of the digital presence or lead generation help to prepare increasingly targeted and interesting strategies.

A further issue to consider is that relating to compliance management in the financial services sector

If you operate in one of the most regulated sectors, and banks and financial services companies of all sizes operate in this context, you tend to worry more and more about risk and compliance management.

These sectors are constantly monitored by the authorities, such as:

➢ MiFID II,

➢ FCA,

➢ PRA,

➢ EDIS,

➢ Basel IV,

➢ GDPR,

➢ RPD

financial services companies are going to employ important resources aimed at limiting risk and respecting an ever increasing number of legal and operational compliance requirements.

As these laws and regulations are constantly evolving, the companies concerned have an urgent need to train financial advisors on updates and how they will affect their work.

All of these change management activities take away valuable time, preventing you from focusing on the economic well-being of your customers.

If we talk about the economics of markets and financial intermediaries, the question is what to do after graduation.

One of the courses that are chosen by students, in their academic training, today is precisely that relating to financial intermediation, obviously it is the case to deepen the issues related to the field of finance, such as that of economics.

The disciplines that concern the areas of economics and finance, among the different possibilities that open up to a young student, are among the most compelling.

Whether we are talking about a three-year degree course, or a master's degree, the branch of the market economy and financial intermediaries is one of the most frequent choices currently for those approaching university.

When choosing, many people ask themselves, of course, what to do after graduation.

So we must also observe this aspect of the question, and I will do it by asking two questions to which I will answer later.

Economics of markets and financial intermediaries, what is it and what is it studied?

Economics of markets and financial intermediaries, does it have job outlets?

Having knowledge of financial phenomena means having an overview of how this matter has a direct influence on the world, and how markets are regulated by the laws it imposes.

Studying the economics of markets and financial intermediaries brings together this decidedly interesting perspective for fans of the subject, and for those who have a natural predisposition to this type of study.

It should be remembered that the term Economics of markets and financial intermediaries, in the current university landscape, gives the name to several degree courses, so in some universities it is indicated as a three-year course, while in others it founds the name of a master's degree course.

Beyond issues related to the nomenclature, the degree courses in Economics of markets and financial intermediaries have the same objectives and ends, and give rise to very similar job opportunities.

These kinds of university courses aim to provide those who choose them with knowledge of financial activities and instruments, with a look towards contracts, but also towards operations on the markets and intermediary management techniques.

The disciplines that are learned in the university path that will lead you to the degree belong to the following spheres:

> ➢ business economics,

> ➢ mathematics,

> ➢ commercial law,

> ➢ financial law,

> ➢ business Finance,

> ➢ activities of financial intermediaries.

What can you do after Economics of Markets and Financial Intermediaries?

A degree course like this prepares the student on subjects studied in a complete and in-depth manner.

These are undoubtedly very important study addresses also for the future and the paths that finance itself will go in the next few years, very important for achieving the basic knowledge to try to enter the world of work.

The world of work based on competition becomes more and more like this, with what this entails on the ethical and moral level but also on the environment and in life itself.

A bankruptcy model which, however, continues and is not questioned except through niches and new models that are less competitive but more respectful of everyone's life.

As this world is more and more competitive, it requires an increasing number of skills.

It is understood that it becomes a necessity to acquire the right skills to move better in the work landscape, and to emerge in one's daily activity, developing one's career.

So there are the Masters in Finance and Management.

A path that provides a Higher Education also and above all on a practical level, oriented to the career of those who participate in the lessons, to allow them to have the indispensable tools to excel in their work, and to deepen everything related to financial discipline.

- ➢ *teachers,*
- ➢ *professionals in the reference sector,*

they help develop strategies but also awareness on this sector that you would otherwise have to start accumulating on your own, with a heavy expenditure of energy.

Even the Career Coaching figures can help you improve your professionalism after completing your university career.

But why choose this type of training?

It is a field in full development as analyzed in the previous pages, which also presents niches and possibilities that are difficult to consider if you are not familiar with the topic.

Many people are looking for experts who can advise them in the financial field without even having basic info, others have a minimum knowledge of this sector, others have a greater one but in all three cases a consultation carried out by an expert who is on your side and you find perfect solutions for your case, it turns out to be a necessity since a consultant immediately knows every market variation and manages to orient the client's real portfolios and needs.

Finance and economy are sectors that can create doubts, especially if you don't know how the market moves, so relying on highly specialized consultants is a way to help you find your way in a hyper competitive and often engulfing environment.

Study addresses and an ever faster economy (thanks to the tech sector) require a high specialization.

Industry and Financial Services: From homeless to billionaire

Have you ever heard the expression "Homeless to billionaire"?

From homeless to billionaire, it is a condition of change that attracts as much attention as it is obvious.

There are also many people who provide advice, but this being a very sensitive issue, it should not be taken only from a propaganda side, as unfortunately often happens instead.

The theme of how to go from homeless to billionaire is embodied by several stories, for example there is that of John Paul DeJoria, who today is an authority on hair products and is also a philanthropist.

He himself made sure to provide advice to those who want to know his story but not only.

Below I want to list the 3 tips for success, devised by DeJoria.

In the meantime, here are some facts:

> ➤ *From homelessness to $ 2.6 billion in assets (Forbes provides the data).*

Very briefly this is the story of DeJoria.

This man was the son of a mother girl, and he had no money in his pocket, while today he controls an empire, made of cosmetics and tequila.

When he lived in poverty, he never lost heart saying to himself that:

<u>"The only direction I can go is up."</u>

And through this real mantra he finally made it.

When dealing with the theme of a personal story, caution is needed, but it must be said that the story of this man is really interesting, as are the three tips on how to be successful in business.

Postcard seller

DeJoria was born in Los Angeles and her childhood did not pass peacefully.

When the parents (an Italian immigrant and a girl of Greek origin) go to separate, he is entrusted to the mother.

The family needs money: to earn something, little John, at 9, sells Christmas cards with his brother.

At the end of high school, he doesn't have enough money to pay for college.

So he starts selling door-to-door encyclopedias.

Recalling that DeJoria period, he said:

"It was one of the most formative experiences of my life.

I learned not to get depressed when faced with a refusal.

When someone closes the door in your face and you don't lose enthusiasm for your job, you know you've won. "

DeJoria gets married very young, but her marriage ends badly.

At 20 he has no job, his wife leaves him and has a three year old to support.

He does not have a home to live in and manages as he manages, here are his words remembering that period:

"I collected plastic bottles - he says - getting something in order to survive.

We slept in the car, washing in a public swimming pool.

In the morning we went to eat eggs and a toast in a cafe that sold them for 99 cents.

And we had dinner in a Mexican restaurant before 17:30 because it offered food at bargain prices. "

Success stories often (not always) have past problems, but that of DeJoria speaks of an ordinary man who, for various vicissitudes, found himself without anything and then rebuilt a whole existence, a new life.

After the divorce, he started working as a seller for Redken, first, and Fermodyl Hair Care, later, companies that put beauty products on the market.

He is fired from both these companies.

But working in this area he meets Paul Mitchel, a barber.

DeJoria turns 30 and is homeless again and together the two find themselves in their pocket for just $ 700.

With this little money they leave to give life to what will then become a billionaire business for them too.

It's 1980, the two create three lines of hair products, with the John Paul Mitchell Systems brand, here's what DeJoria says about that period:

"I spent the first few weeks of launching the business on the street again. An investor promised us half a million dollars, but eventually disappeared.

We went on anyway.

I had no money and went back to live on the street. We placed the first products at the city's beauty salons, selling them door to door. "

The idea is reflected in the market and the first customers begin to spread the word.

Then comes the first major distributor.

Two years pass before the final statement, but from here on the road is downhill to DeJoria.

Although there is no shortage of personal suffering: shortly after the launch of the brand, his partner Mitchell dies of cancer.

The company currently generates $ 1 billion a year in revenue and DeJoria has interests in other sectors as well.

Among the most famous, the Mexican tequila Patrón, which he bought in 1989 with his friend Martin Crowley and which today sells two million cases per year.

So far I have illustrated the personal story that is intertwined with the entrepreneurial one of DeJoria, but I still haven't told you about the three tips that this entrepreneur provides to those who feel disheartened but not only.

Here they are, but first a maxim always applicable:

➢ *If you expect free food to fall from the sky, you will be bored early and won't go far. Get out there and do something, get involved.*

In fact, this is the philosophy of life that has continued DeJoria throughout its journey.

Currently, at 74 years old, and with a career of this type behind him, he can afford to advise those who are beginners how to achieve success.

Here are three tips revealed by DeJoria to CNBC.

➢ *Get ready for the doors in your face (and keep your spirit up)*

"You will knock on many doors and many will close in your face. Some will not like your products, others your company. You won't like others as a person.

To be successful, you must maintain the same enthusiasm and the same security in your vehicles that you had at door number 1 also at door number 59 ".

Rejection is part of the game. All the older ones have seen several or even many doors closed in the face, at least it will have happened only once.

Accepting the possibility of failure will help you be resilient, explains DeJoria.

> *Constantly perfecting your product*

> *Always remember: you don't want to win in the product business.*

> *You want to win in the reordering one.*

> To be successful, according to DeJoria, the product you are going to put on the market must convince beyond expectations. If you can, then you won't sell the goods one time: people will call you back to get more.

This is DeJoria's second tip: to work hard to offer the best product, always.

> *Doing good is good for you and your work*

In 2011, DeJoria founded the Peace, Love & Happiness Foundation, a foundation that intended to promote humanitarian and environmental protection projects.

> *The last tip is not to base your success on the dollars that you can earn or on the power obtained*

DeJoria writes:

"I have experienced very hard moments in my life. This made me grateful for what I have now and for being able to return what I got.

I always get great joy from it: it's my way of paying the rent to this planet and sharing what I have with the less fortunate. "

A perspective that, for DeJoria, will help you but will also help your work:

"If a company wants to stay healthy, it can't just think about the results of the day. By helping others, you are creating future customers and building employee loyalty.

Consumers like to connect with people and companies who know how to donate their time to others, who save the planet, who make the difference. "

It is often said that money brings money.

That is wealth that brings more wealth.

And in many cases it is so.

Yet there are stories, and there are many, of billionaire entrepreneurs who started from the lowest step.

To then reach the highest one. DeJoria's is one, but it is not the only one, in fact, I want to show you further success stories made by people who started practically from scratch to reach the peak of important careers.

Here are five more to follow.

These stories teach us that with talent, determination and a bit of luck everyone can overcome great obstacles and achieve success.

I will start with Howard Schultz, CEO of Starbucks.

Currently Schultz has accumulated a fortune of 2 billion dollars and its chain of coffee shops has shops scattered everywhere.

Still, the Starbucks CEO grew up in a residential complex for destitute citizens: his family could not afford a home.

He was able to find the turning point thanks to sport: by virtue of his skills as a football player he entered the University of Michigan.

He then began working at Xerox, a multinational printers and copiers, and then set up a business and opened a Starbucks store (which at that time only had 60 stores).

He stands out until he became CEO of the company, and it was 1987. Under his leadership, the company reaches 16 thousand points of sale worldwide, your advice? There he is:

"Get your hands dirty. Listen and communicate with transparency. Tell your story and don't let others tell it for you or define you.

Draw inspiration from those who have real experiences to tell you.

Link their stories to your values. Make tough choices: action matters. Seek the truth and lessons in every mistake.

Be responsible for what you see, listen and achieve. "

Another success story of those who recently left to reach high levels is that of Leonardo Del Vecchio, CEO of Luxottica.

Today Del Vecchio returns to the ranks of the richest men in the world with a fortune of 15.3 billion dollars.

Last of four brothers and fatherless (the parents were fruit merchants from Barletta), he spent his childhood in an orphanage.

Start working as a worker in a metal engraving factory. At the age of 23 he opened a small shop of glasses frames in Belluno.

Today it is one of the largest eyewear distributors in the world, and which competes with brands like Ray-Ban and Oakley, here's what it says:

"I have based my whole life on true values, these are the most important thing. They are the demonstration that you can do business in Italy and be honest at the same time.

Of course, nobody likes paying taxes. But I like to sleep soundly. "

A name that perhaps you would not expect is that of Ralph Lauren, an American designer, who also started with very few resources and is now well known in his brand.

Today Lauren has assets of $ 7.7 billion. And to think that this man's career begins as a salesman in a shop.

Aveva la sua residenza nel Bronx ed è figlio di ebrei immigrati dalla Bielorussia, lui entra prima nell'esercito e poi viene assunto come commesso da Brooks Brothers.

It was during this last work experience that he came up with the idea: to create wider ties and with a more colorful style. Start putting them into production.

His dream came true in 1967: he sells ties worth $ 500,000 and here's what he says:

"People often ask me how a Bronx Jew could make trendy ties for an elite, without having money and not belonging to a high class.

I answer that I succeeded because I had learned to dream ".

The fourth name is Micheal O'Leary, CEO of Ryanair.

His company today has a profit of 523 million euros. An unexpected career for O'Leary who starts his career as a bartender and with the savings earned pays the university, while continuing with the management of a newsstand.

After graduation he worked as a tax consultant.

The turning point of his life came in 1987 when he had a meeting with Tony Ryan founder of the company that O'Leary will take over seven years after that meeting.

Since 1994, it has undergone a series of transformations in this low cost airline, taking an idea from the United States and applying it to corporate management, O'Leary says:

"I started from small businesses: I opened at 7 in the morning and closed at 11 in the evening. That's how I learned how to run a business. Not on the books. "

The fifth story is that of Renzo Rosso, CEO of Diesel.

Rosso was born into a family of farmers. Start working driving the family tractor. He became passionate about fashion at the age of 15, producing his first jeans with his mother's sewing machine.

Renzo Rosso, owner of Diesel, achieved success starting from very little and nothing. Today he has $ 3.5 billion in assets and says:

"Being fashionable and trendy means investing continuously in new things and people, embracing risks.

Without taking into account the economic situation and the crises ".

But so far I have only told you about successful men who have left little or nothing, to follow I also want to report stories of women who are often overlooked who have made the climb to success, the women I will consider are from different eras and many have gone down in history.

The women who sit in the button rooms are to date as analyzed even a little while ago, still too few, and this is a fact, but in recent times our ears have got used, fortunately, to hear about female entrepreneurship, an entrepreneurship that is not young, however, and which has spanned the history of industry, technology and the entire market for years and years.

And if today the success in squad is no longer news as it was some time ago, it is due to those pioneers who have been leading the way over the years, although sometimes their stories have not found a place in the history books.

It is therefore necessary to talk about some of these women, to tell their story and the path that led them to success, how they changed the world with their innovations, and how they paved the way for those who came after them.

I want to start with Mary Katherine Goddard, a woman who in Rhode Island in the United States in 1766 became the first female publisher in America. Goddard assumed command of her brother's newspaper when the latter went abroad for business, and held the helm of command for 10 years.

But to this primacy adds a second, Goddard was the first woman to become director of an overseas post office, this happened in 1775.

Instead two years later she was removed from her position by the director general in favor of a political ally, and this sparked protests from Baltimore citizens who were against this measure.

A petition was also organized then to get her back, but this stance on citizenship was unsuccessful.

All this did not go down in history, what made it recognized in history was having printed the first copy of the Declaration of Independence which included all the names of those who had signed it.

Mary Katherine Goddard, after the post office, continued to work as a printer and a seller of books and other goods, until her death in 1816.

Why do we include women on this list of people from scratch?

Not only for equality but also because the female has much more difficulty in establishing herself in areas and in general in the world of business and work, paying the gender gap (still today) but which in the past was even more intense than what we live today, so they started from scratch, even if they could have been bourgeois once it was unthinkable that a woman would work outside the home.

The second name on this list is that of Lydia Pinkham who in 1875 managed to transform her natural home remedies into a real job.

The secret was a winning marketing strategy, she introduced her products to women and educated them to recognize health problems.

The success was remarkable so much that it was recognized as a champion of women's health in a time when the needs of these were not listened to by the medical community and were not calculated at all (certainly there was no gender medicine at the time!).

Its product (known and appreciated) was Pinkham's Vegetables Compound, a mix of roots, herbs and alcohol, which served to relieve menstrual pain and menopausal symptoms for which it was aimed exclusively at women.

She started by distributing her natural remedies to her friends, relatives and neighbors, but her notoriety increased when some strangers contacted her for her recipe.

At this point, together with her three children, Lydia started packing and selling her remedy to a wider audience.

As a result of this event, he opened the company in the cellar of his home in Lynn, Massachusetts. The product was later advertised in many American newspapers, and the company remained active until 1968, when it was absorbed by a larger industry.

Another important woman was Madam C.J. Walker. The history of this woman makes her, with good probability, one of the most successful women of the whole 20th century.

She spawned her empire from nothing, really going at a disadvantage since her parents were slaves, and she was orphaned at only 7 years old.

In 1905 he invented the recipe for a hair product that can soften and heal the scalp. Her name was Madam Walker's Wondefull Hair Grower, she came up with the idea because she personally had a disease that caused her to lose most of her hair.

After the success at home, in the United States, the one arrived in Central America and the Caribbean.

Its success was such that, in the second decade of 1900, exactly in 1917, it held the first international meeting of women entrepreneurs in Philadelphia, entitled "Madam C.J. Walker Hair Culturist Union of America Convention ".

We move from America to Italy and to Luisa Spagnoli who in 1907 founded one of the best-known Italian companies together with her husband, giving life to one of the most loved products ever.

If the name of this entrepreneur is known today as a fashion brand, its history will surprise you, given that Spagnoli founded the Perugina company, and with it the invention of the "Kiss", a must have that has marked industrial history of Italy, the famous chocolate.

Following the withdrawal of her husband from the company, she took over the corporate helm. He concentrated on improving the conditions of employees, creating homes, company kindergartens and promoting a rather revolutionary work ethic for that period.

As for the fashion brand, it was founded four years after his death by his son Mario, keeping in mind the innovative technique through which Spagnoli supplied himself with angora wool, practically combing the rabbits that she raised, instead of skinning them .

Another important female name was that of Ma Perkins along with that of Virginia Payne.

She worked in the times when the radio occupied a place of honor in the heart of the Americans, the actress Virginia Payne played the character of Ma Perkins in more than 7,000 episodes, going to attract the attention of the listeners with her kindness and genuineness.

Perkins was a self-sufficient widow who ran a carpentry shop, offering advice to those seeking help. Virginia Payne made her radio debut with Ma Perkins in 1933, and the show continued to air on NBS and CBS until 1960.

Payne died in 1977, 11 years before seeing her radio alterego introduced into the Hall of fame dedicated to radio.

Then there was Brownie Mae Humphrey (Brownie Wise), a name that is not well known, but a universally known brand redeems it for this woman.

Brownie Wise was a single mother who, in 1950, realized that Tupperware would sell more in parties organized in private homes than in stores or better then in stores.

Her marketing strategy was spot on and Earl Tupper, the inventor himself, appointed her vice president of his company.

In 1958, however, Mr. Tupper fired her when the press indicated her as responsible for Tupperware's success.

Wise died in 1992, but her sales strategy continues to be applied in many companies.

After this devalued and punished woman (something that often happens not only in companies and towards women) here is another, Ruth Handler. You may know her if you are fond of dolls.

Ruth Handler is the story of Barbie's "mom".

With her idea of white and blonde doll with blue eyes, Handler has profoundly changed the way girls play, and dream, as well as leaving an indelible mark on western culture as it is understood.

The idea behind Barbie's success came to her creator by watching her daughter play.

Ruth noted, that the little girl preferred to play with paper dolls that looked like adults.

Her husband did not support her intuition, but in 1959 she made her debut at the New York toy fair.

Ruth and her husband were already selling some Mattel products, and in 1967 Handler became president of Mattel, a role she held until 1974.

Her legacy continues to grow today as Barbie makes Mattel take over $ 1 billion a year.

A name you may not know (another name) is that of Oprah Winfrey, born in Mississippi in 1954, Oprah Winfrey lived in poverty, but this did not stop her and she managed to complete her studies in communication all over the world. state university of Tennessee.

His beginnings took place on the radio, where he made his debut in 1983 in a morning talk show, after a few months his program began to become unpopular and from there his career took off towards the great celebrity he still embodies today.

Currently this woman is the producer and conductor of her show, the famous The Oprah Winfrey Show, but she is also the founder:

> *from the O magazine,*

> *the Oprah.com website dedicated to the female lifestyle.*

In addition, its association Oprah's Angel Network raises around $ 70 million which it totally donates to the coffers of non-profit organizations.

Oprah also started a production company, Harpo Productions Inc., and co-founded cable television for women Oxygen Media.

In simple and straightforward words there seem to be no limits to what this fantastic businesswoman can do.

There is still a woman who deserves to be mentioned on this list, she is Sara Blakely who in the late nineties wanted to produce women's socks that were modeling and that left the foot free.

He then created the concept of support underwear, which wrote the word end to the oppression of pantyhose.

To test her prototypes, Blakely used her own body.

He decided to personally test the products, in an environment that he considered this prudence superfluous.

In 2000 Blakely founded Spanx, today a millionaire company, also thanks to Oprah Winfrey who nominated her during one of her shows.

Starting from nothing material and from a situation of social unease that is punitive in nature are two unfortunately still very present today.

Many women and men go through these discriminatory forms by focusing on their ideas and personalities to make their way in contexts that appear (and I emphasize appear) very distant from them.

Not all billionaires were born with shirts as you can guess from the stories I have reported so far by extrapolating them from various information collected, from articles dedicated to them.

Even the way of saying "I made myself" may seem like a commonplace, but it has its roots in realities.

Many people through incomparable determination and perseverance, there are people all over the world who have thus managed to overcome inequalities by achieving success.

Here are additional people who were born poor and became billionaires.

Altrad was born in a nomadic tribe in the Syrian desert to a poor mother who was raped by her father and who died when he was young, Altrad was raised by his grandmother, who forbade him from attending school in Raqqa.

Altrad attended it anyway and, when he came to France to attend university, he did not know French and lived by eating only once a day.

He later obtained a PhD in computer science, and went to work for some major French companies until he bought a bankruptcy scaffolding company which he transformed into the world's leading scaffolding and concrete mixer manufacturer, the Altrad Group.

He was named Entrepreneur of the year in France and globally.

Then there is the figure of Troutt, who grew up with a bartender father and who paid for his studies at Southern Illinois University by selling life insurance.

He accumulated most of his assets through the Excel Communications telephone company, which he founded in 1988 and went public on the stock exchange in 1996.

In 1998 Troutt merged his company with Teleglobe with a $ 3.5 billion deal.

He is currently retired and invests in racehorses.

Another name (this time very well known) is that of Abramovich born poor in southern Russia. Orphaned at the age of two, he was raised by an uncle's family in a subarctic region of northern Russia.

As a student of the Moscow Auto Transport Institute, in 1987 he managed to start a small company that produced plastic toys, with which he managed to finance an oil company and make a name for himself in this sector.

Then, as the sole head of the Sibneft company, he managed to complete a merger that made it the fourth largest oil company in the world. The company was sold to the state titan Gazprom in 2005 for $ 12 billion.

As known, this tycoon bought Chelsea Football Club in 2003 and bought the largest yacht in the world, which cost him nearly $ 400 million in 2010.

Another lesser known entrepreneur is Shahid Khan who once washed dishes for $ 1.20 an hour.

He is currently one of the wealthiest people in the world, but when he arrived in the United States from Pakistan, he did a job as a dishwasher while attending the University of Illinois.

Khan currently has Flex-N-Gate, one of the largest private companies in the USA, as well as the Jacksonville Jaguars football team and the English Fulham football team.

Instead the founder of Forever 21 Do Won Chang shortly after he moved to America he worked as a caretaker, gas station attendant and bartender.

The couple: Do Won Chang and Jin Sook before Forever 21 did not do so well.

After arriving in America from Korea in 1981, Do Won did three jobs simultaneously in order to make ends meet. Together with his wife Jin Sook he opened their first shop in 1984.

To date, Forever 21 is an international empire that boasts 480 stores and achieves approximately 3 billion in revenues per year.

Another highly controversial name, given the ArcelorMittal trial that took place after the massacre in Italy where many workers died, delivers the Indian steel tycoon Lakshmi Mittal to the news but he too had started from scratch, and was of humble origins.

A 2009 BBC article reports that the CEO and chairman of the board of directors of ArcelorMittal, born in 1950 from a poor family in the Indian state of Rajasthan: he laid the foundations of his fortune in two decades guaranteeing most of his business in the equivalent of a discount in the steel sector.

Today Mittal manages the largest steel producer in the world and is a multi-billionaire.

There is another figure worth mentioning, that of the luxury tycoon Francois Pinault who put a brake on his schooling leaving high school in 1974 after being bullied because he was poor.

Pinault is now the face of the Kering fashion conglomerate (ex PPR), but once she had to leave high school because she was heavily teased for her economic condition.

As a businessman, Pinault is known for his predatory tactics, here she is exposed to follow:

buying smaller brands for a fraction of their value when the market collapses.

Subsequently this aggressive tycoon set up PPR, which owns high fashion houses including:

- ➤ *Gucci,*
- ➤ *Stella McCartney,*
- ➤ *Alexander McQueen,*
- ➤ *Yves Saint Laurent.*

Today, it also acquired Christie's, the largest auction house in the world.

Another name is that of trader George Soros who survived the Nazi occupation of Hungary and worked as a porter in London.

In his early teens, Soros pretended to be the godson of an employee of the Hungarian Ministry of Agriculture to remain safe during the Nazi occupation of Hungary.

While in 1947, he fled the country to live with his relatives in London.

He managed to stay at the London School of Economics as a waiter and porter.

After finishing his studies and after graduation, he worked in a gift shop before getting a job as a banker in New York.

In 1992, his famous bet against the Pound managed to make him a billionaire.

Then there is the magnate Li Ka-shing who after the death of his father had to leave school to support the family and fled from mainland China to Hong Kong in the 1940s, but his father died when he was 15 years old, and so took responsibility for the maintenance of the family.

In 1950, he managed to start his own company, Cheung Kong Industries, which started producing plastic and then headed towards the real estate sector.

There is also in this group of people who "made themselves" Sheldon Adelson who left college and grew up sleeping on the floor of a Boston apartment block Adelson's son, a taxi driver, grew up in Dorchester, Massachusetts, and he started selling newspapers at the age of 12, explains Bloomberg Businessweek.

Forbes says that after dropping out of City College of New York Adelson:

"He built a fortune by managing vending machines, selling advertisements in newspapers, helping small businesses to go public, building condominiums and organizing trade fairs."

Adelson lost almost all of his assets during the 2009 crisis, but recovered a large portion of it in subsequent years, currently manages Las Vegas Sands, the largest casino company in the world, and Forbes considers him to be the largest political backer.

Oracle co-founder Larry Ellison instead left the university after the death of his foster mother, and did occasional work for eight years.

Born in Brooklyn, New York, as a single mother, Ellison was raised in Chicago by her uncles.

After his aunt died, he left university and moved to California to do casual jobs for the next eight years.

He later founded the Oracle software development company in 1977, now one of the largest IT companies in the world.

He recently announced his plan to step down from Oracle's CEO to become CTO and executive director.

Then there is the story of Guy Laliberté who was a fire eater before founding the Cirque du Soleil, currently very famous as known.

At the beginning of his career, Laliberté the Canadian busker played the accordion, walked on stilts and ate fire.

Afterwards he tried his luck and bought a one-way ticket from Québec to Los Angeles for the circus company that in Las Vegas would become the Cirque du Soleil, of which the busker is now AD.

Finally, I cannot fail to mention the founder of WhatsApp Jan Koum who, at the beginning of his entry into the world of work, cleaned the floors.

Koum was born in Kyiv, Ukraine.

At 16, he and his mother left for California, where they got an apartment through government subsidy. To survive, he swept the floors in a local shop.

According to the Independent, Koum learned self-taught computer science.

In 2009, he co-founded the largest instant messaging service WhatsApp, which was then acquired by Facebook in 2014 for $ 22 billion.

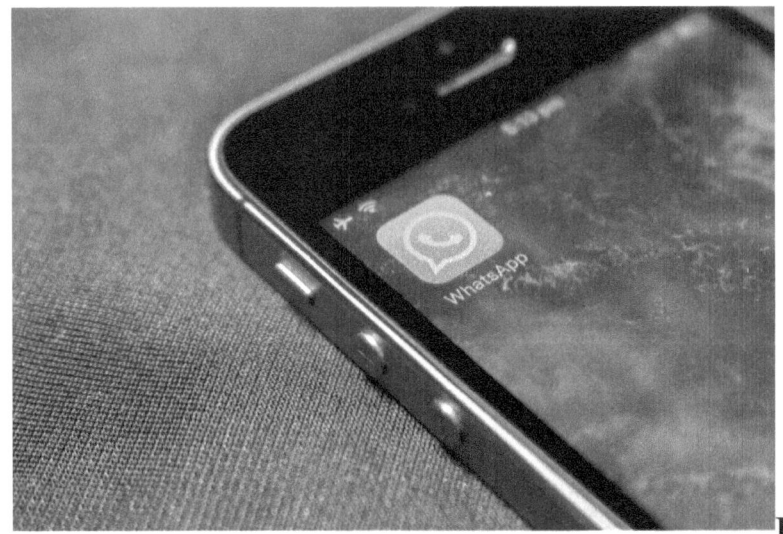

Stress   Less
Success: how to forget stress and achieve success

Never heard the mantra:

Less stress, more success

I guess so, even if the theme of stress appears much more followed abroad than in some countries of Europe such as Italy for example, and this is bad because this social phenomenon is widespread and looking for solutions would be appropriate.

There is a woman who has been looking for them, and not only her, proposing to get their hands on these methods never seen before to help you achieve greater success and without having to stress you.

How many tips have you received in your life?

Tips aimed at making you optimize your time by avoiding the stresses that arise at work, whether you are an employee or an employee or you are an entrepreneur or entrepreneur.

Tips that often represented a hole in the water.

Take everything you've been taught about maximum performance and put it aside, right now.

Often we ourselves make a business bigger than it actually is, we are certainly conditioned to do this, and such induction is itself the cause of stress.

You probably think you have to endure a lot of stress and struggle to achieve success, but what you've been taught in the past has created the blocks that currently hold you back.

Have you ever noticed that when you are at your best, you are in the flow, things happen and manifest themselves effortlessly?

You are not struggling to think positively and work harder.

You are serene, confident and creative.

There is a woman who has been able to give a face to the inductions that drag us culturally, this woman is Janet McKee who has managed to define this state of success without stress and can show you how to invert your internal switch anytime, anywhere to free your personal power and your productivity.

There have been executives, such as the Fortune 500 who almost died of a severe breakdown and then managed to rise from his ashes, Janet McKee is dedicating her life to helping others succeed in entrepreneurship and work without stress.

Stress-free success will leave you with the incredible ability to raise your thoughts, your emotions and your energy in a way that can be useful to the whole of your life that needs to flow easily rather than accumulating stress.

Now is the time to discover the surprising secret that will change and improve your life forever. This proposes McKee.

The author has created a book that has precisely this title: Stress less Success and when you read it you will certainly find it very stimulating, you must also know that this text focuses on various aspects that can be summarized as holistic practices but also strongly anchored to reality .

Stress involves us all and it does it particularly in the world of work that asks for more and more competitiveness going to affect personal energy resources and developing as we now know, as a real disease.

Treating the onset of this condition beforehand becomes essential and here is what McFee offers in its illuminating pages:

> *How to combat negativity and fear of the present.*

> *Because positive thinking is not the answer and can even be harmful.*

> *How to quickly recognize gifts in any challenge and turn them into opportunities.*

> *How to discover your incredible power to achieve a life of passion, purpose and prosperity.*

> *How to find the only goal you will ever need to achieve everything you want and much more.*

When you are busy or committed to achieving your goals in various areas of your life but you don't see results, you can get discouraged.

You can easily feel as if the goal at the end of the path was not possible to reach and therefore was never within reach.

Hope can easily vanish in an attempt to achieve certain goals and therefore you feel that happiness and fulfillment will never be your reality.

A woman who invites us not to surrender to this negative dimension must certainly be listened to, also taking into account the fact that this book and the teaching that follows it, represent a better way to achieve your goals so that your probability of reaching them is greatly improved.

I want to start from an example that I will list to you in specific points below:

> *You are waiting for that new job that has been promised you*

> *You have goals and desires associated with such work, which you are passionate about*

> *You start to elaborate thoughts like: I will be able to move house, buy a new means of transport, I will have more money at my disposal*

> *Add to this your sentimental situation which can transform and stabilize with a new job.*

Here, this is the worst way to start a new adventure, expectations are not wrong, expectations are desires, they can also be used to improve and also improve material conditions, the mental approach is wrong.

Thoughts make me sick, I repeat, not the expectations that are legitimate but the way of conducting thoughts by putting a series of stakes to desires and fixing them.

There is no worse disappointment than those who plan expectations.

This approach feeds the spiral of stress, it is a fact and if you do not get (for any reason, which may or may not depend on you) what you thought in this way, in the times when you thought it, here it is triggered the spring of disappointment and stress.

It is logical (and in the order of things) that you can set goals, entering even more into the merits of the topic, because you think that achieving them will make you happy and fulfilled.

Stai ancorando la tua stessa felicità declinandola a ciò che puoi ottenere, prova a guardare questo aspetto

Another good exercise you can do is ask yourself why you want to achieve certain goals.

Do this until you get to "find" the core of the main feeling because that's the essence of what you're actually looking for.

I give another example, always following the lesson that McFee provides and provides us, the answers that are provided to her are of this kind:

> ➢ *I want a new home.*

Then she asks why they want a home.

A further answer may be the following:

> ➢ *Because I want more space for my family and to move to a better neighborhood.*

It is understandable how the interlocutor describes at this point the questions from McFee continue, once again asking why and a subsequent answer is the following:

> ➢ *Because it will bring us a feeling of space, comfort and safety.*

And this is the conclusion.

McFee translates (rightly) this as follows:

It's a feeling that you want and believe that the goal will make it easier for you to feel freedom, comfort, joy and fulfillment.

According to McFee, the problem lies in the fact that if you are unhappy while you are struggling and struggling to achieve these things, this represents a serious impediment.

You feel stressed by working so hard that you not only affect your emotional well-being, but you also go to work on your physical health and you do not dive into the moment, you limit yourself to dissatisfaction by canceling (automatically) the positive aspects of the present experience, the pressure social exists but it can be faced in a thousand different ways.

In summary and in conclusion:

How much will you be able to enjoy your new home if you are sick and tired ?.

But the truth is that the home will not come or take much longer to reach through stress and struggle because you start being weakened.

In reality you have to improve your state of happiness and contentment at the start, and the things you want to achieve (and more) will come easily and you will enjoy them instead of getting there tired and weakened in your own life energy.

The cornerstone to achieve your goals and therefore a successful life is based on your level of joy and fulfillment, not the opposite, the goal if there is no initial state of serenity becomes a top that appears unreachable and these feelings (with attached thoughts) hurt you.

Obviously you will not develop an attitude overnight (that is to think positively) you will have to train your mind to structure a sense of mental, emotional and physical well-being with an attached positivity while working towards your goals, no matter what they are.

Another attitude to avoid and which unfortunately is also a basis often, is that of not believing that you can control what others do or say or the things that happen around you, and therefore allow your thoughts and emotions to be dictated from others.

Nobody controls anyone, if you act as the controlling you get stressed.

However, you have complete management over the thoughts you choose and the feelings you feel and this has a direct impact on what really happens around you. And this is empowrment.

The problem is that happiness is elusive for many people, you will tell me, and in fact it is true. In today's world, everyone lives at a level of stress, fear and anxiety that destroys the quality of their work, relationships and health.

People continue to struggle and struggle only to get stuck and frustrated because they cannot understand how to reach the standard of living they desire.

When you are stressed and struggle starting from this condition, you block both your overall view of the phenomena that are around you and that concern you, and the solutions and opportunities that can present you on your way.

McFee often talks about how to combat negativity and develop a consistent and sustainable mentality of passion and positivity.

When you start living at a high level of hope and positive anticipation, things flow better in life and your mood helps you move faster on the path to success.

Just pay attention to it.

If mentally and spiritually, in your mood, you are fine, the things that happen to you seem to fit perfectly, like pieces of a puzzle.

This is not a coincidence.

Athletes who win and very creative people always do it, they are looking for a state of emotional well-being and have shown that they are also the most skilled people in the world according to McFee.

When you are in a positive high-energy inner area, you are actually open to allowing good things to appear in your life.

To do this and therefore to take action, it is important to prepare practices and habits and then implement them to continuously feed positive energy and enthusiasm.

What do you do to achieve this state of affairs?

Do you like to go to bed early and feel comfortable in bed so as to wake up rested and calm?

Do you like saying some prayers or meditating in the morning and then having good intentions for a day?

Do you love singing your favorite music in the shower and dancing in the kitchen while having breakfast?

Do you love running in the morning and listening to your favorite music in the meantime?

It seems absurd that few and simple actions can constitute the (solid) basis that allows you to face life better by reducing stress?

Well, living the moment, savoring it, making it joyful, means loving and loving each other, it does not foresee pain or disturbance for you or for those around you.

Ok, I'm having fun with you here, you will think ...,

but in the meantime I ask you if it's not nice to smile?

The truth, however, is that I'm not kidding and what I mentioned, the activities I mentioned to which I also add nature walks, are the way you choose to start the day.

And, when you start the day like this, the rest of the day is better.

You will be more productive because you will feel happy and full of energy, so things happen that take you further on the path to success.

You will intuitively feel that there is something true in what I am telling you.

You have to remember that the days when you get up and put your toe out of bed is the moment when things start so live them.

You say, as the day goes by, that you should have stayed in bed, that things are not going, that the day is lost etc ... etc ... It is what they say:

"Getting up on the wrong side of the bed."

This is not just a coincidence; is reality.

Because as soon as you put your first foot on the ground you start a downward spiral of thoughts that become more and more negative until you find yourself venting hatred and avoiding it is instead essential.

You will drag your anger out onto the street and by going to work you will find that your biggest customer has canceled the contract.

Sounds like a catastrophe right?

What you may not want to hear is that you created this by allowing your energy and positivity to go up in smoke.

If, on the other hand, you could intentionally and convincingly repeat positive thoughts about your day before you even got out of bed and you will be more likely to laugh at yourself and say to yourself:

I'm glad I removed something unpleasant first so that the rest of my day can be positive.

So smile.

The positive elements cannot be overshadowed by stress and a discouraged attitude!

When you get to work, even if your biggest customer calls to say that they are thinking of canceling the contract, you will think that it is only one customer, however important and this will spur you to understand and understand the reasons why the customer has decided to cancel the contract, you have the opportunity to improve yourself, because waste makes you improve.

Or you will be able to propose (starting from a positive basis) the solution that your client wanted and you will save the contract, as a pessimist you would not have succeeded.

There are mental shots, those for which you will be able to deal positively with any stress situation, we speak only of course, other problems such as discrimination and verbal and psychological violence are not included in the list of such treatments since they are carried out by people who are not they know how to put themselves in someone else's shoes and try to cowardly crush others.

Employing the power of your imagination is another strategy that has a similar and very powerful effect.

If you can imagine that your goals have already been achieved and have the feeling as if they were already, then you already start to experience that good feeling that you hope to preserve and take care of once you reach your goals.

This practice must be exercised and requires that you can develop a skill that of the imagination that our society teaches us to disperse when we go from being children to growing up.

It is a skill that needs to be focused, and that is capable of bringing you into that area of positivity, which increases your chances of success.

At this point McFee asks again and asks the interlocutor:

what is your real goal?

The main goal that everyone must set before everyone else is to cultivate high thoughts and emotions, whatever happens.

You must develop happiness habits and practices that lead you to your inner place of well-being and support you as frequently as possible.

Learn how to feed your passion, positivity and purpose.

There are many seminars in which the issue of stress is addressed, in these places experts from the sector and other sectors such as the corporate work for example take turns.

Another good basis is to connect the knowledge of the individual by communicating with those who live the experience of stress with the consequences to which this leads.

The most popular advice (and it's good advice) is:

Make the most of your energy without weakening it and without being knocked down.

Before you immerse yourself in such teaching, feeling joy is essential to gaining the freedom of stress-free success.

Always remember that you are not the first (you will be the last) person who experiences stress, people get stressed and fight while trying to achieve their goals I said it, I wrote a little about it.

They believe that once they reach the goals of a new job, a new home, new relationships and cars, they will have achieved happiness (as in a war and this is also a wrong attitude).

And I have already written about this too ...

The truth is that if you are unhappy while walking, you put a brake on your goals.

Stress tends to take up much more space than it should occupy.

Mind you, when there is a negative event we tend to magnify it, the same thing applies to stress.

Looking inside and admitting that we help fate to be nefarious, certainly not easy, but not doing so leaves us stalled with negative thoughts and emotions that also pollute our body, in fact today medicine recognizes the correlations between stress and physical diseases.

Why continue self inflicting malaise?

In conclusion of this ebook, as you will be at this point maybe still with some questions, I want to offer you 15 habits that will help you to overcome stress, making your life a little smoother.

When you are in the vortex of stress, some good practice can help, so I propose some:

> _To breathe._

Breath is the link between our mind and our body.

When we are stressed, the breaths become short and assiduous; on the other hand, when we are relaxed, our breaths are slow and deep.

When you feel stressed, concentrate on your breathing for a few minutes, using your abdomen to inhale and exhale.

> _Employ a to-do list._

We often tend to be stressed because the burden of having to do many things acts on us, in this case a to-do list is appropriate that helps to empty the mind and allows us to organize our activities.

> ➤ *Plan the day.*

You only need 10 minutes in the evening to take stock of the activities to be completed the next day, and if you can't think of it positive, the next day you will take into account the things you managed to do and those that require you to take different times, you will have learned something on you.

> ➤ *Write in a diary that is yours alone.*

Le ragioni per cui tenere un diario sono tante, ma qui voglio concentrarmi su una in particolare, la mente ha idee, non funge da magazzino, se diventa "ripostiglio" ti stressi, scrivi le tue idee, portale avanti e una volta realizzata una passerai al percorso con quella successiva.

> ➤ *Evita il multitasking, fai una cosa per volta.*

Multitasking is praised but it is a mental slavery that generates stress that easily becomes physical illness, it is not a nice way of being in life, indeed it is bad.

You don't have to care what others think try to do one thing at a time: you will rediscover the flavor of individual activities and the pleasure of immersing yourself in them.

> ➤ *You tend to build order around you.*

The disorder of the spaces in which we are, whether personal or working, does not help, on the contrary, it becomes a "foothold" for stress as the chaos of our mind is reflected in the chaos.

> ➤ *Give up unnecessary things (which are also often harmful).*

This point is connected to the previous one, if you learn to tidy this will help you get rid of old useless things.

Here I am not talking about objects that have an affective value, but those that chain you, and we all know that such objects exist.

> ➤ *Learn where to place things.*

Learn to keep things right.

Chaos arises and expands when you start to place our things where it happens; give it a try for a week and then continue on good practice.

- ➤ *The turnout towards social and media falls.*

Ask yourself a question.

If you are stressed, does Facebook help you calm down or amplify it?

The second, so getting used to going constantly on FB or watching TV when you are already stressed out, is a good practice, also because if you are not the one controlling the social networks, they will control you.

- ➤ *Don't check email*

How many newsletters do you receive?

And how many notifications?

How many times a day do you check your inbox? 5? 10? 50 times a day?

Staying connected will not help you be less stressed.

- ➤ *Do you need something? Ask!*

It seems stupid but it is not in fact there are many people who either impose or shut up not to ask, both of these practices cause stress so they are a sign of little love for themselves. Learn to ask.

- ➤ *Question yourself.*

As you will ask others, you must ask yourself questions too, pride and narcissism create serious pathologies, did you know?

Quite different from self-confidence, having awareness means asking oneself by going in depth without being satisfied with the mainstream answers, which are almost always not even answers.

Finally, read the advice given to you by Coaches like McFee who has been working on stress for years and what this disorder can generate.

www.ingramcontent.com/pod-product-compliance
Lightning Source LLC
Chambersburg PA
CBHW030649220526

45463CB00005B/1700